A STUDY
IN SILVER

A STUDY IN SILVER

A second collection
of bridge stories

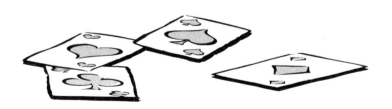

David Silver

Master Point Press
22 Lower Village Gate
Toronto, Ontario, Canada
M5P 3L7

(416) 932-9766

Canadian Cataloguing in Publication Data

Silver, David, 1934-
A Study in Silver: a second collection of bridge stories

ISBN 0-9698461-5-0

1. Contract bridge - Fiction. 2. Canadian wit and
humor (English).* I. Title

PS8587.I272S78 1998   C813'.54   C97-932424-6
PR9199.3.S54S78 1998

Cover design: Sue Peden
Interior design: Olena Serbyn
Editor: Ray Lee
Hand analysis: Linda Lee

Printed and bound in Canada

1 2 3 4 5 6 7   07 06 05 04 03 02 01 00 99 98

To Bruce Gowdy:
a good sport,
a great bridge player,
and a wonderful human being
away from the bridge table

PUBLISHER'S NOTE

The more perceptive among our readers will notice that all of the stories in this book derive at least a part of their plot-line or characterization from certain of the classics of literature and the screen. They may be interested to compare the bridge versions with the originals, which are:

CONTENTS

The Legend of Zelda

THE S-FILES

REQUEST PERMISSION TO TRANSMIT.

** *Permission granted, GRID 4321, Circuit A4655* **

AM IN POSSESSION OF TWO TERRAN LIFE FORMS, PLEASE IN-STRUCT.

** *Describe* **

SUBJECTS CORRESPOND TO EARTH SURFACE SCAN #43321, BIPEDS, APPROXIMATELY 40 MARSECS IN HEIGHT, 600 AND 990 MARPACS IN MASS, NO OBSERVABLE SEXUAL ORIENTATION. EARTH DESIGNATIONS "SILVER" AND "HAMBLY". UNLIKE PRE-VIOUS CONTACTS, THESE SUBJECTS SHOW NO REVULSION OR FEAR AT MY APPEARANCE.

** *Interrogate* **

SUBJECTS SAY THAT I LOOK AND SMELL LIKE AN ORDINARY BRIDGE PLAYER EXCEPT FOR MY COLOUR AND MY SIX EXTRA LIMBS. ALSO THAT I EXCRETE IN GREATER QUANTITIES.

** *Information request: Bridge Player:* *[Searching data] [Background transmission] ---Cards---Games---Social*

*problems---Deviant Behaviour---[EOT] ; Interrogate re scientific status
of civilization-- technological advances* **

SUBJECTS REFUSE TO DISCUSS ANYTHING BUT RECENT EXPE-
RIENCES AT BRIDGE TOURNAMENT. REQUEST PERMISSION TO
COMPLY---IMMINENT DANGER MUTUAL DESTRUCTION OF SUB-
JECTS IF CONFLICTS NOT RESOLVED.

**Affirmative **

SUBJECT "SILVER" CLAIMS TEAM GAME LOST BECAUSE SUB-
JECT "HAMBLY" MISPLAYED FOUR HEARTS. HAND FOLLOWS.

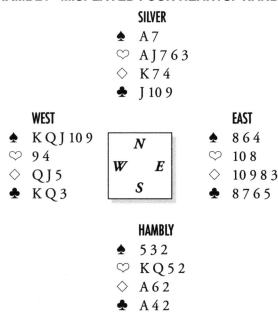

                         SILVER
                    ♠ A 7
                    ♡ A J 7 6 3
                    ◇ K 7 4
                    ♣ J 10 9

  WEST   **EAST**
♠ K Q J 10 9   ♠ 8 6 4
♡ 9 4   ♡ 10 8
◇ Q J 5   ◇ 10 9 8 3
♣ K Q 3   ♣ 8 7 6 5

                         HAMBLY
                    ♠ 5 3 2
                    ♡ K Q 5 2
                    ◇ A 6 2
                    ♣ A 4 2

SUBJECT "HAMBLY" DUCKED THE KING OF SPADES OPENING
LEAD AND WON THE CONTINUATION WITH ACE IN THE DUMMY.
SUBJECT "HAMBLY" THEN DREW TRUMPS ENDING IN DUMMY
AND TOOK A CLUB FINESSE. LATER, SUBJECT ""HAMBLY"
TOOK ANOTHER CLUB FINESSE. SUBJECT CLAIMS THAT THE
REPEATED CLUB FINESSE MAKES CONTRACT 75% AND HIS LINE
OF PLAY WAS CORRECT. HE LOST ONE SPADE, ONE DIAMOND,

AND TWO CLUBS. ANALYZE PLEASE.

**Contract is 100% certain. Impossible to fail when South is declarer **

SUBJECT "HAMBLY" REQUESTS CLARIFICATION.

**Not necessary: winning line obvious **

RECOMMEND CLARIFICATION, SUBJECT "HAMBLY" IS ROLLING ON THE GROUND AND MAKING UNINTELLIGIBLE SOUNDS.

**Clarification: Duck king of spades, win continuation. Draw trumps ending in South hand. Ruff South's last spade in the dummy and then play A, K, and another diamond. Even if West unblocks QJ of diamonds and East wins third round, declarer ducks club lead to West. West must return club into declarer's tenace or yield ruff and sluff. Location of missing club honour irrelevant to outcome **

SUBJECT "HAMBLY" CLAIMS TEAM GAME LOST BECAUSE SUBJECT "SILVER" MISPLAYED SEVEN SPADES. HAND FOLLOWS.

HAMBLY
- ♠ A K 6 4
- ♡ 8
- ◇ Q 7 6 5 3 2
- ♣ A 4

WEST
- ♠ 10
- ♡ K 10 3
- ◇ J 9 8 4
- ♣ J 10 8 6 3

EAST
- ♠ 9 3 2
- ♡ Q J 4 2
- ◇ 10
- ♣ Q 9 7 5 2

```
      N
  W       E
      S
```

SILVER
- ♠ Q J 8 7 5
- ♡ A 9 7 6 5
- ◇ A K
- ♣ K

BOTH SUBJECTS REFUSE TO DISCUSS THE BIDDING. SUB-
JECT "SILVER" (SOUTH) WON THE CLUB LEAD, DREW
TRUMPS AND THEN PLAYED THE ♢A AND ♢K. HE CLAIMS
THAT THE BAD TRUMP SPLIT AND THE 4-1 DIAMOND DISTRI-
BUTION MAKES THE HAND IMPOSSIBLE TO MANAGE. WITH
ONLY ONE DUMMY ENTRY, THE DIAMONDS COULD BE ES-
TABLISHED, BUT THERE WAS NO WAY TO RETURN TO CASH
THEM. ANALYZE PLEASE.

*Declarer wins club lead, cashes queen of spades and ace of dia-
monds. When both opponents follow, declarer claims 13 tricks   **

SUBJECT "SILVER" REQUESTS CLARIFICATION.

*Are you certain that you have captured sentient life forms?   **

[SEARCHING DATA] THESE TWO ARE DEFINITELY IN THE
HIGHEST CATEGORY OF EVOLUTION ON THIS PLANET. EACH
CLAIMS THE OTHER IS THE LOWEST LEVEL OF TERRAN IN-
TELLIGENCE.

*Which is correct?   **

[SEARCHING DATA] BOTH. URGENTLY RECOMMEND CLARI-
FICATION OF GRAND SLAM CLAIM AS SUBJECT "SILVER" IS
TURNING PURPLE AND HIS VITAL SIGNS ARE VERY WEAK.

*Declarer wins ♣K in hand, cashes ♢A and ♠Q and travels to
dummy with ♠A. Then ♣A is cashed and declarer discards ♢K. A
diamond is ruffed in hand and declarer returns to the dummy with
king of spades and ruffs another diamond, establishing the suit.
Later, he can ruff a heart with dummy's last spade and cash three
more diamonds **

SUBJECT "HAMBLY" CLAIMS TEAM GAME LOST BECAUSE
SUBJECT "SILVER" MISPLAYED THREE NOTRUMPS. HAND
FOLLOWS.

HAMBLY
♠ 5 2
♡ J 10 5
♢ A 7 3
♣ Q 8 7 6 3

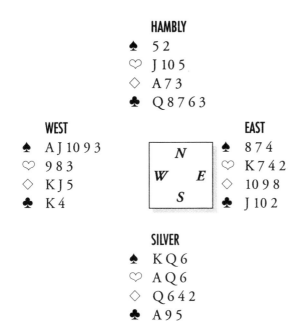

WEST
♠ A J 10 9 3
♡ 9 8 3
♢ K J 5
♣ K 4

EAST
♠ 8 7 4
♡ K 7 4 2
♢ 10 9 8
♣ J 10 2

SILVER
♠ K Q 6
♡ A Q 6
♢ Q 6 4 2
♣ A 9 5

SUBJECT "SILVER" (SOUTH) WON THE JACK OF SPADES LEAD AND ATTEMPTED TO PLAY ACE AND ANOTHER CLUB TO THE QUEEN. LHO PLAYED THE KING OF CLUBS ON THE ACE. EAST COULD NOT BE PREVENTED FROM GAINING THE LEAD BEFORE DECLARER COULD SET UP NINE TRICKS. SUBJECT "SILVER" CLAIMS THAT WEST MADE AN EXPERT PLAY TO BEAT AN ODDS ON GAME. ANALYZE.

**Negative: terminate subject "Silver" immediately **

SUBJECT "HAMBLY" REQUESTS THAT SUBJECT "SILVER" NOT BE TERMINATED.

**Assure subject "Hambly" that a better partner can be found by select-ing any terran life form at random **

SUBJECT "HAMBLY" IS AFRAID THAT WHEN SUBJECT "SILVER" IS TERMINATED, SUBJECT "HAMBLY" WILL BECOME THE WORST BRIDGE PLAYER ON TERRA.

**Subject "Hambly" shows signs of rudimentary intelligence: retain subject "Silver" and proceed with interrogation. Clarification of three notrump contract follows: declarer wins spade lead and leads low club towards dummy's queen. if LHO rises with club king then nine tricks are on top: one spade, four clubs, three hearts and one diamond. Success of heart finesse is assumed for contract to be made: if LHO ducks club king, declarer wins queen of clubs in dummy and ducks a club into LHO's now singleton king. A diamond switch forces a low diamond from dummy in order to preserve ace for a dummy entry. Ace of clubs drops RHO's club jack and clears the suit **

SUBJECT "SILVER" POINTS OUT THAT LHO MIGHT HAVE THREE CLUBS TO THE KING AND THEN EAST WILL GAIN THE LEAD WITH HIS DOUBLETON JACK, LEAD A SPADE THROUGH DECLARER AND THE CONTRACT WILL FAIL. CLARIFY.

**The probability of RHO's holding club doubleton is 34%, just as for LHO. But if LHO holds three clubs king he is less likely to hold a five-card spade suit. If LHO has only four spades contract cannot be beaten with a spade lead. This line of play far superior to any other; further explanation beyond mental capacities of subject "Silver" **

SUBJECTS REQUEST THAT WE PLAY WITH THEM IN THE SUMMER NATIONALS. SUBJECTS CLAIM THAT WITH THEIR EXPERIENCE AND OUR ABILITY WE CAN WIN SPINGOLD EASILY.

**Negative: probability of winning anything with "Silver" and "Hambly" approximately 0.00000001: proceed to Summer Nationals and register for Life Masters Open Pairs. **

AFFIRMATIVE: YOU DO NOT THINK THEY WILL NOTICE OUR APPEARANCE?

**[Searching data] Tell them we are part of the Blue Team [EOT] **

A Study in Silver

Being a reprint from the reminiscences of Wright X. Cardinal, B.A., late of the Department of Correctional Services

In the year of 1978, I took my degree of Bachelor of Arts and proceeded to gainful employment with the Ontario Civil Service. I was duly attached to the Department of Correctional Services as counsellor to clients of the Parole Board, preparing them to re-enter society. The field brought honours and promotion to many, but for me it held nothing but misfortune and disaster. My counselling career ended in 1990 when my most promising client, who had been, upon my written recommendation, released thirty years early from Her Majesty's prison system, went directly from the prison gates to the nearest branch of the Bank of Montreal. Once there, the unfortunate wretch calmly made a substantial withdrawal, undeterred by three security cameras and an electronic alarm system.

I was despatched, accordingly, to the land of unemployment, and arrived a month later, with my career prospects irretrievably ruined, but with pecuniary support from a paternal government sufficient to allow me to spend the next few months in attempting to improve them. I decided then and there to earn my living by transforming my avocation, bridge, into my occupation.

I continued, however, to spend such money as I received more freely than I ought. So alarming did the state of my finances become, that I soon realized that I must either give up my new profession and seek a more regular source of income, or make a complete alteration in my style of living. Choosing the latter alternative, I began by making up my mind to give up my lodgings and to reduce my eating habits.

On the very day that I had come to this conclusion, I was standing on the street corner, cap in hand, when someone tapped me on the shoulder, and turning around I recognized young Hambly, against whom I had played recently in a team match. The sight of a friendly face, coupled with his willingness to buy lunch, persuaded me to spend some time in conversation. I recounted the history of recent events and complained of the lack of comfortable lodgings at a reasonable price.

"That's a strange thing," remarked my companion, "You are the second man today who has used that expression to me."

"And who was the first?" I asked.

"A former bridge partner of mine," he replied. "His family abandoned him a few months ago when his circumstances were reduced by what, he claims, was an involuntary retirement from the teaching profession. He was bemoaning himself this morning because he could not get someone to share with him some nice rooms which he had found, the rent being beyond his own means alone."

"By Zia," I cried, "if he really wants someone to share the rooms and the expense, I am the very man for him."

Hambly looked rather strangely at me over his coffee mug. "You don't know Professor Silver yet," he said. "Perhaps you would not care for him as a constant companion. He is a little queer in his ideas — an enthusiast in the more obscure areas of bridge — an avid and undoubtedly expert player, yet I cannot recall his ever winning anything."

Hambly kindly condescended to act as intermediary and a bargain was soon struck with the singular Professor Silver. The latter was to conclude the arrangements and move into the rooms, while I was to dispose of my furniture and join him a week later. I arrived seven days later at 4441 Butcher Street, where I first made the formal acquaintance of Professor David Silver, late of Mohican College.

I entered a lofty chamber, lined and littered with countless books. Broad, low tables were scattered about, which bristled with bridge magazines, scholarly articles, charts, and graphs. Three computer screens were flickering in the half-light, and I could just make out a shadowy figure peering myopically at a series of numbers flickering across the screen. At the sound of my entrance he glanced around and sprang to his feet with a cry of pleasure.

"I have it," he cried, bounding towards me with a printout in his hand. "An algorithm which computes the optimum bidding to describe a 6-6-1 distribution."

Had he discovered a gold mine, greater delight could not have shone on his features. He composed himself, shook hands and then returned to his discovery.

"Think of it, a mere 42 bids to memorize, and one need never be at a loss to describe any hand containing two six-card suits! I must submit a monograph to *Bridge Canada* immediately. I see you have been in Seattle recently."

"It is interesting, mathematically, no doubt," I answered, wondering how he could possibly know that I had just returned from the Nationals, "But practically...." I stopped, realizing I was wearing my 'I Had a Whale of a Time in Seattle' baseball cap.

"Why, my dear Cardinal, it is the most practical discovery since the invention of the unusual notrump. You will recall the critical swing hand from the Creed-Lebovic match of 1949, when the Creed team lost because the primitive bidding methods used at the time precluded their finding the optimum contract, one club doubled. Not having my methods available, they defended four spades and consequently lost the match."

Hambly's warnings had led me to approach my new mode of living with some little apprehension, but Silver was certainly not as difficult a man to live with as I had feared. He was quiet in his ways, and his habits were nocturnal. He was completely obsessed with bridge, and possessed a remarkable library of hand records, antiquarian bridge texts, and bridge magazines in every conceivable language. Yet he rarely touched a card, content to theorize on bidding and play. "It wouldn't be fair," had been his demurrer to my invitation to play one evening.

The extent of his dedication was made clear to me one evening when I happened to observe that the government had fallen and that an election was therefore imminent. It transpired that he knew nothing of current events, and he admonished me for telling him the news.

"You see," he explained, "I consider that a bridge player's brain is like an empty attic, an attic that you may stock with such furniture as you choose. A fool takes in all the lumber of every sort that he comes across, so that the knowledge that might help him play bridge gets crowded out, or at best is so jumbled up with other things that he has difficulty laying his hands upon it. Now the skilful player is very careful indeed as to what he takes into his brain-attic. He will have nothing but the tools which may help him win bridge matches, but of these he has a large assortment, and all in the most perfect order. It is a mistake to think that that little room has elastic walls and can distend to any extent. It is of the highest importance, therefore, not to have useless information elbowing out bridge knowledge. Most truly great bridge players know nothing of the world beyond the bridge table; that is what distinguishes them from the mass of mediocrity."

During the first few weeks, we had many callers, some of whom I recognized as prominent bridge players, and Silver would commandeer the use of our living room for the duration of their visits.

"I have to use this room as a place of business," he said. "These people are my clients." Mystified, I asked what line of work he pursued.

"Well, I have a trade of my own; I suppose, in fact, that I may be the only one in the world. I'm a consulting bridge expert, if you can understand what that is. In the bridge world, we have numerous playing professionals — but you know that, you aspire to be one yourself. When these fellows are at a loss for a double-dummy solution, or a bidding system needs honing, and all other avenues are exhausted, they come to me. Most frequently, my task is to apportion blame when there has been a disaster at the table. They lay the hands before me, describe the bidding, and I am generally able, with the help of my knowledge of the history and theory of bridge, to set them right.

"That letter you are holding is from Rodwell — a minor play problem involving a simple criss-cross, strip and endplay, stepping-stone squeeze, for which he begged a solution. A trifling problem and I was pleased to oblige him as he needed it to complete the manuscript of his book. Of course there will be no reference to my role in the solution; I much prefer to remain anonymous."

I chanced at this moment to glance through our window at the street outside, and observed a small, swarthy, bearded man who was walking slowly towards our building.

"Silver, there is a strange-looking man approaching our door,"

I said, pointing him out. "What do you make of him?"

"Aside from the obvious facts that he is the assistant rabbi of a small Reform congregation in Hamilton, that he is fifty-two years old and has six children, I can see nothing unusual about him," responded Silver as I answered the urgent knocking at our door."

"Is Professor Silver home? Ah, hello cousin David — I need a favour from you. Two of my congregation, avid bridge players, are on the verge of divorce because of some disagreement during their last game. They have, at my insistence, agreed to let you settle their quarrel. May I bring them in? They're waiting in the car."

Although this case did not appear likely to present even a one-pipe problem to the great man, it seemed that the appeal to family ties would not fall on deaf ears. Silver graciously agreed to render what assistance he could, and the little man returned accompanied by a man and a woman in late middle age, whom he introduced as Irving and Mary. Mary was insistent that Irving had misplayed a three notrump contract, which had been made at the other twelve tables; Irving maintained that there were only eight tricks to be had, given competent defence. I was pressed into service as a fourth as Professor Silver led the way to our bridge table. His intention was to play the hand out and adjudicate the quarrel by means of a practical demonstration.

CARDINAL
- ♠ K 2
- ♡ K Q 4 2
- ♢ 10 9 8 6 3
- ♣ K 5

SILVER
- ♠ A 4 3
- ♡ A 5 3
- ♢ K 4 2
- ♣ A 7 4 2

The bidding proceeded with Silver, as dealer, opening with 1NT. I raised to three, and Irving led the ♣J. Silver went up with dummy's king upon which Mary deposited the queen. The ◇10 was led from dummy and Mary swiftly went up with the ace; on this trick Silver followed low and Irving showed out, discarding a spade. A low club came back; Silver ducked this, but he was forced to win the third round as Mary discarded a small diamond. Now the Professor tried to run the heart suit but they broke four-two and he could only come to eight tricks. The full hand was:

CARDINAL
- ♠ K 2
- ♡ K Q 4 2
- ◇ 10 9 8 6 3
- ♣ K 5

IRVING
- ♠ J 9 7 5
- ♡ J 10 7 6
- ◇ —
- ♣ J 10 9 8 3

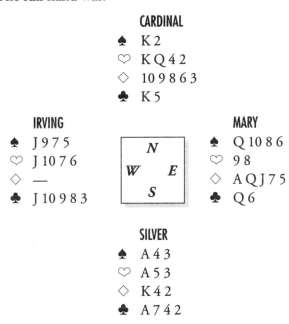

MARY
- ♠ Q 10 8 6
- ♡ 9 8
- ◇ A Q J 7 5
- ♣ Q 6

SILVER
- ♠ A 4 3
- ♡ A 5 3
- ◇ K 4 2
- ♣ A 7 4 2

"With both red suits breaking badly, there are only eight tricks available. I cannot see what there is to discuss, let alone argue about," he pronounced as the last trick was turned.

It was, perhaps, fortunate that Silver's hearing was failing (while still vigorous, he was even at this time in our acquaintance no longer a young man) and he was unable to hear what Mary was muttering. He did, however, catch the word 'squeeze' and responded to the allusion.

"It's elementary; you have to rectify the count to execute a squeeze, but declarer has no idle cards left after the clubs are cleared, so the hand cannot be made. Perhaps," he added, with the unfailing courtesy that he always showed to the fair sex, "you would care to make the attempt yourself?"

They switched seats and once again, Irving led the ♣J. Dummy played the king and Silver unblocked the queen. The ◇10 was led from dummy, Silver going up with the ace and Irving discarding a spade. Silver returned a club. So far, the play had been identical. However, instead of ducking, Mary won the ♣A, cashed the ◇K and played another diamond from her hand to the Professor's ◇J.

Irving, however, had been having great difficulty playing to the diamond tricks. Forced to retain his last two clubs to prevent Mary's simply conceding a club to him and establishing her ninth trick in that manner, he had discarded spades. This was now the position:

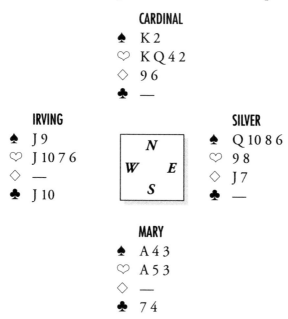

CARDINAL
♠ K 2
♡ K Q 4 2
◇ 9 6
♣ —

IRVING
♠ J 9
♡ J 10 7 6
◇ —
♣ J 10

SILVER
♠ Q 10 8 6
♡ 9 8
◇ J 7
♣ —

MARY
♠ A 4 3
♡ A 5 3
◇ —
♣ 7 4

The professor sank into thought, emerging with a low spade, which Mary won in dummy. She called for the ◇6, and looked triumphantly at the great man, who had won the ◇7 but was not looking happy about it.

"Well, Professor?" she enquired.

"I really beg your pardon!" said Professor Silver, who had ruffled everyone's temper by bursting into an explosion of laughter. "Of course, you all see the predicament this charming lady has engineered for me? If I cash the last diamond, I squeeze poor Irving in the round suits; if I play anything else, Mary still executes the same ending by cashing the top spade. I suppose you could call it a suicide squeeze without the count!

"But let me explain further. I didn't mean that the hand couldn't make on a misdefence. I meant what I said, which was that you couldn't make it on a squeeze because you couldn't rectify the count. An expert, like Cardinal here, would have foiled your plans by returning a heart rather than a spade at trick six; that would have altered the timing sufficiently to destroy your squeeze.." He smiled sardonically, gazing up at the ceiling.

Irving, however was spluttering furiously. "But it does still work! All declarer has to do is to win the $\heartsuit$A, and play two more hearts; you have to keep two diamonds, or Mary just concedes one, so you have to come down to three spades. Now Mary can play three rounds of spades and endplay you to lead away from the $\diamondsuit$J, establishing dummy's nine for the ninth trick! Come on, dear, let's get out of here. I don't think much of this so-called professor's powers of analysis!"

They left the room, arm-in-arm, saying more unkind things about their host as they left with the rabbi.

"I trust, Cardinal, that you grasp the significance of my not making three notrumps?" He seemed surprised at my negative response and continued. "The task at hand was not to provide a demonstration of my superior analytical powers, but to reconcile an estranged couple. Before they came they were hostile to each other, whereas now they have a new target for their anger, a common enemy, so to speak. They will live happily ever after."

"Good heavens, Silver, you surely don't mean that you deliberately misplayed the hand in order to make them angry at you instead of each other? I find that hard to believe..."

"Have you not heard me say that when you have eliminated the impossible, whatever remains, however improbable, must be the truth? What would have happened if I had proven one of them to be correct? The winner would have had a weapon with which to beat the other and the bridge partnership would precede the marriage into dissolution. I would have thought, however, that even a player of your limited perceptual acuity would have realized that the hand is cold on any defence."

(It took several hours, but eventually I was able to satisfy myself that the Professor, as usual, was absolutely correct. The analysis, which is complex in the extreme and involves various squeezes and endplays, is left as an exercise for the reader. WXC.)

Nothing eventful happened for days after this incident. I, being short on funds, could not play bridge and rarely stirred from our chambers, while Professor Silver appeared to have fallen into a black depression, sitting, often for hours, staring into space. He complained bitterly, in his rare moments of lucidity, that there were no interesting bridge hands left, that all had been played years ago, and that no challenges worthy of him remained. One afternoon, I found myself staring at a wall plaque which I had noticed earlier in passing but to which I had given little attention or thought. The inscription read:

*To Professor David Silver with Grateful Thanks
on the Occasion of his Early Retirement.
From the Students and Staff of Mohican College, June, 1988*

This struck me as a singularly worded testimonial. I was on the point of inquiring of the Professor as to the circumstances which had led to its presentation when there was a loud knocking at the door. I hastened to open it and a large, gray-haired man rushed past me.

"It's terrible, David, you're the only man who can help us," he cried, striding across the room. The lethargy which had beset my companion of late disappeared in an instant.

"My dear Cardinal, may I present President Oldham of Mohican College, my old mentor," he exclaimed, delightedly. "Bill, pray enlighten us as to your present difficulties; I shall be delighted to render whatever assistance may lie within my poor ability."

"David, do you remember the proposal you sent to the Canada Council just before you retired? It was titled *Digigrade Manipulation: A Proposed Experiment in Alternative Dexterous Control Mechanisms.*

"Indeed, I composed it at our Christmas party right after I boasted that I could teach students to play bridge with their hands tied behind their backs."

"That's the one! Well, to our collective astonishment, not only was your project approved, but we received a five-figure grant towards the research. Well, it is not college policy to turn down funding, for any reason whatsoever. So Professor Modo set up a class of twenty-four of your ex-students from Bridge 101 in a lab where they have been learning how to play bridge using only their toes to hold and manipulate the cards. They are, of course, already well-skilled at opening beer bottles with various and sundry parts of their bodies, so are quickly becoming quite proficient at card handling.

"But the government is demanding an interim report, and we desperately need your expertise to solve some of the technical nomenclature problems. For example, do you still call them bridge 'hands'? If you're not in dummy, where are you? There is a host of similar conundrums that only you can decipher — you must help us. Of course, the grant will more than cover your usual fee."

Galvanized by the prospect of professional activity, Silver stood erect and paced eagerly while he listened to this appeal from his old colleague. When President Oldham had finished, Silver nodded assent immediately, and turned to me with a familiar gleam in his eye.

"Rouse yourself, Cardinal," he said. "The game's afoot!"

THE GRAY-HEADED LEAGUE

When I glance over my notes and records of Professor Silver's cases in the early 90's, I am faced by so many that present strange and interesting features that it is no easy matter to know which to choose and which to leave. Of course, the details of some (like the bizarre incident of Dr. Norton's cue-bid, and its scandalous aftermath) must remain concealed from the public for some time yet. Others will perhaps be described here in some future chronicle, since they demonstrate the unique powers of logic and reasoning that gave the professor his stature in the bridge world. For example, from 1992 alone, I could recount the curious affair of the Hexagonal Squeeze, the adventure of the Trumpless Dummy, and, perhaps as strange as any, the singular Case of the Granite Brewery, where the professor was able to reconstruct an entire hand after determining which brand of beer declarer had ordered after the game.

One afternoon in the apparently endless winter of that same year, I had spent some hours attempting to supplement my income in a two-penny game. I had fallen behind in the first few pivots, but was poised to recoup it all when my partner unaccountably went down in a grand slam which was cold on a trivial backwash squeeze. Luck had, evidently, abandoned me for the day, so I returned early to the rooms which I shared with Professor Silver. I found him deep in conversation with a stout, middle-aged man with a shock of prematurely gray hair. With an apology for my intrusion, I was about to withdraw when Silver pulled me into the room and closed the door behind me.

"You couldn't possibly have come at a better time, my dear Cardinal," he said cordially.

"I'm afraid that you are busy. I'll wait in my room."

"Not at all." Turning to his client, Silver continued "Mr. Bird, this gentleman is the famous bridge player, Wright Cardinal. He has assisted me in many cases and I have no doubt that he will be of the utmost use to me in yours also.

"Now, Cardinal, Mr. MacDonald Bird here has been good enough to call on me today and to begin a narrative which promises to be one of the most singular which I have listened to in some time. Perhaps, Mr. Bird, you would have the great kindness to recommence your story. I ask you not merely because my friend Mr. Cardinal has not heard the opening part but also because the peculiar nature of the story makes me anxious to have every possible detail from your lips. The facts as I understand them so far are unique."

I turned my attention to Mr. Bird who produced from his pocket not, as I expected, a bridge hand, but an advertisement from a newspaper. I took the paper from him and read as follows:

ATTENTION GRAY-HEADED BRIDGE PLAYERS

On account of the bequest of the late Commodore Vanderbilt, of New York, the Gray-Headed League now has another vacancy open which entitles a member of the ACBL to a salary of $600 a week for purely nominal duties. All gray-headed bridge players who are life masters, overweight, and above fifty years of age, are eligible. Apply in person on Monday, 10 a.m., at the offices of the League, 120 Bay Street, Suite #1204.

"What on earth does this mean?" I asked, after twice reading this extraordinary announcement.

Silver chuckled. "It is a little off the beaten track, isn't it? It appeared in the *Globe & Mail* just two months ago."

"I have never heard of this Gray-Headed League. I'm sure that

Mr. Bird here was the only applicant."

"On the contrary, my dear Cardinal. With the age of the average life master hovering statistically at 63.5 years, and given the sedentary life that bridge players lead, I'm sure that there was no dearth of candidates for the position."

"That's correct, Mr. Cardinal," said Mr. Bird, mopping his forehead. "I had been out of work for some months, so I don't mind telling you I was downtown bright and early on the appointed day. I have never seen such a sight as greeted me upon my arrival. From six states and three provinces, every bridge player who had a gray hair in his head had shown up to answer the advertisement. There were more life masters lined up on the sidewalk than had attended the entire ten days of the Toronto Nationals. But surprisingly, the line progressed very quickly and I soon found myself in an office being interviewed.

"There was nothing in the office but a couple of wooden chairs and a plain desk, behind which sat a small man whose hair was even grayer than mine. He said a few words to each candidate as he came up, but he always managed to find some fault which would disqualify them. However when my turn came, the little man was much more favourable to me than to any of the others and when I sat down, he immediately cleared the office and closed the door."

"Looking intently at my hair, he exclaimed 'I have never seen anything so fine. It would be an injustice to hesitate. You will, however, excuse me for taking an obvious precaution.' With that he leaned forward and tugged on my forelock until I yelled with pain.

"Apologizing vehemently, the little man explained 'We have numerous applicants try to deceive us with wigs and dye, but I can see you are just the man we are looking for.' He congratulated me, and went to the door and announced loudly that the position had been filled. Loud protestations intermingled with imaginative obscenities surged up the stairwell but the little man locked the door and returned to his desk. He explained the conditions of employment.

" 'You have to be in this office every evening between 7:30 and 9:00, and every afternoon from 12:30 to 2:00, including weekends. You must be in the office at all times during those periods or you forfeit the whole position forever. The Trust is very clear on this point — you don't comply with the conditions if you budge from the office during that time. The work consists of solving bridge problems: hands will be supplied for your analysis, your solutions will be submitted to me as you complete them, and new ones will be given to you.'

"By the time I started that evening, I had quite persuaded myself that the whole affair must be some great hoax or fraud. However, supplied with keys, I let myself into the office at 7.30 and found everything as promised. The odd thing was that I could not dial out on the telephone, although it rang occasionally. It was always the little man who merely greeted me and hung up. Two bridge problems had been left for my analysis, and I began work. At the end of the week, my employer paid me a visit and left an envelope containing $600 in cash.

"I have been working diligently on these same two bridge problems for weeks now, but I fear that they are beyond my powers of analysis. Surprisingly, when I questioned the little man about one hand, he announced that he neither played the game nor had any interest in it, being merely the paid agent of the Trust. He assured me that my progress was sufficient and that he and the officers of the League had every confidence in me. My apprehension, however, increases in direct proportion to my tenure, so I have come to you for help. You are as famous for your discretion as for your analytical skills."

Appealing at the once to Professor Silver's vanity and his charity had the desired result. His demeanour changed from amusement to intense interest as he perused the first of the two bridge problems.

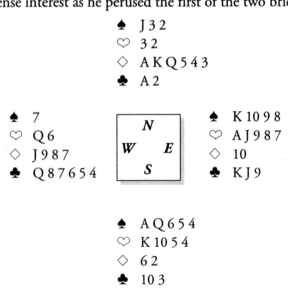

```
              ♠  J 3 2
              ♡  3 2
              ◇  A K Q 5 4 3
              ♣  A 2

♠  7                              ♠  K 10 9 8
♡  Q 6          N                 ♡  A J 9 8 7
◇  J 9 8 7    W   E               ◇  10
♣  Q 8 7 6 5 4    S               ♣  K J 9

              ♠  A Q 6 5 4
              ♡  K 10 5 4
              ◇  6 2
              ♣  10 3
```

"East opens the bidding with 1♡, South overcalls 1♠, and is raised to 4♠ by North. The opening lead is the ♡Q, and the problem is to make ten tricks, assuming the best defence," offered Bird.

"What do you think of declarer's chances, Cardinal?" asked the Professor. "Clearly East must employ the Merrimac Coup, winning the ♡A and shifting to the ♣K, removing dummy's entry before the diamonds can be established. Declarer wins the ♣A, and a low spade is led to the queen, which holds. What now?"

"Well, with the bad splits in both spades and diamonds, declarer must lose four tricks: two spades, a heart, and a club. If you play ace and another trump, East sets you with the king and ten. If you cash ♠A and play on diamonds, East ruffs in on the second round and declarer will still lose a heart in the endgame. There is no escape, it seems."

"Perhaps, Cardinal, you should spend less time bemoaning your bad luck and more on studying the technical points of the game. 4♠ is assured against any defence."

Smiling at Bird's and my astonishment, the Professor continued: "Surely the winning line is obvious. After winning the ♣A, declarer finesses the ♡10, and ruffs a heart in dummy before playing a spade to the queen. Now he can cash the ♡K, disposing of dummy's club, ruff a club in dummy and lose only two more trumps to East."

"But what if East lets declarer win trick 1?" I ventured.

Looking like a man who had just experienced a severe blow to the abdomen, Silver replied. "You are right, we must assume expert defence. We shall now cross to the ♢A, finesse the ♠Q, and play another high diamond, forcing East to ruff. He returns a club to our ace, and we play the ♢Q, throwing a club as he ruffs with his trump trick. Not a problem, you see, Cardinal..."

"But, Silver, cannot East return the ♠K at this point, removing dummy's last low trump and cutting us off from the diamond suit for ever?" I enquired meekly.

"Ever alert, my dear Cardinal, I see," the professor snarled in reply. "The ordinary expert would have fallen into that trap, of course, but the exceptional bridge player will think ahead and avoid the snare that has been set for him. He ignores the trump suit, playing high diamonds immediately at tricks two and three. East ruffs and returns a club to dummy's ace, and we play the ♢Q, pitching a club as East ruffs in again.

"Playing hearts will do him no good, and if he tries a club we give up a heart and cross-ruff the hand, so a trump return is perforce his only option. We shall allow a low trump to run around to our jack, ruff a diamond, draw his last trump, and eventually ruff a heart to dummy to enjoy our winning diamonds. The ♠K return is even easier to deal with — win the ace, cross to the ♠J, and ruff a diamond, eventually again returning with a heart ruff to the remaining diamonds."

He stared at me as if daring me to challenge his intellect further, but I had exhausted my imagination on behalf of the defence.

"Well done indeed, sir!" I cried, as Bird attempted desperately to copy down the analysis in his notebook.

"Elementary, my dear Cardinal. As I am always pointing out to you, the one requisite for successful declarer play is the ability to see all four hands."

"Well, I never!" said Mr. Bird, rejoining the conversation at this juncture. "I thought at first you had done something clever, but I see there was nothing in it after all."

"I begin to think, Cardinal," said Silver, "that I make a mistake in explaining. *'Omne ignotum pro magnifico'*, you know, and my poor little reputation, such as it is, will suffer shipwreck if I am so candid. Do you have another hand, Mr. Bird?"

Our visitor quickly presented the following hand:

```
              ♠  K 4 3
              ♡  J 6 3
              ◇  A 2
              ♣  A K 7 6 5

♠  Q J 7          ┌──────────┐          ♠  9 8 6 5 2
♡  5              │    N     │          ♡  4 2
◇  K 9 7 4        │  W    E  │          ◇  Q J 10 6
♣  Q J 10 9 2     │    S     │          ♣  8 4
                  └──────────┘
              ♠  A 10
              ♡  A K Q 10 9 8 7
              ◇  8 5 3
              ♣  3
```

"South is to make 7♡, on the lead of the ♣Q," he said.

"A great contract," I commented, "but the hand is hopeless: the best declarer can do is give up a diamond and ruff one in the dummy. If this is a team game I suggest North and South try to sneak out of the building without comparing scores — the opponents at the other table will be in a small slam, easily making."

"You see, Cardinal, but you do not observe," said Silver, as Bird maintained a respectful silence. "The grand slam is cold on the lie of the cards. You, of course, would stake all on the club suit since, obviously, if they split 4-3 you get two diamond discards, one on the king and one on the fifth club. But really great declarer play overcomes bad breaks and surmises a possible, if not probable, lie of the cards which will produce the requisite number of tricks.

"The sensible thing to do is to win the club in dummy and immediately ruff a club in hand. Declarer draws trumps ending in the dummy, and cashes the ♣K; when the bad break dooms the obvious line of play, he ruffs a club and then plays two more trumps, bringing about this end position:

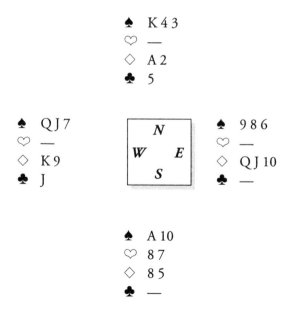

          ♠ K 4 3
          ♡ —
          ◇ A 2
          ♣ 5

♠ Q J 7   ♠ 9 8 6
♡ —   *N*   ♡ —
◇ K 9 *W*   *E* ◇ Q J 10
♣ J   *S*   ♣ —

          ♠ A 10
          ♡ 8 7
          ◇ 8 5
          ♣ —

"South now leads the ♡8, shedding a small diamond from dummy, and in the process squeezing West in three suits and East in two. If

West discards a diamond, East has to throw a spade or declarer can execute a simple double squeeze by cashing the ♢A, the ♠A, and the ♡7 in that order. But after East's spade pitch, declarer cashes the ♢A, returns to the ♠A and leads the last trump, squeezing West in the black suits.

"The ending is more interesting if West discards a spade on the ♡8, since East must now shed a diamond to keep a spade guard, and the lead of the last trump again destroys the defence. West dare not release the ♣J for fear of dummy's five nor can he discard another spade — if he were so foolish, declarer would cash the ♠A10 and dummy's ♠K would be trick thirteen. So poor West, perforce, discards the ♢9, dummy the now useless club, and East finds himself contemplating Hobson's Choice: throwing a diamond sets up declarer's eight for the thirteenth trick, and discarding a spade establishes dummy's three. A moderately interesting problem — it would probably cause a delay of several seconds if I had to work it out at the table."

Bird was simultaneously scribbling notes and thanking the professor as he rose to leave. Silver escorted him to the door, taking the opportunity as he did so to ask Bird if he were married. The reply being negative, Silver smiled, closed the door and slumped into his favourite chair, lost in thought. After some minutes of silence he snapped his head up, fixed his cold blue eyes directly on me and asked "What time is it?"

The question startled me, for Professor Silver does not normally dwell in a universe that is bounded by space and time. I noted from our wall clock that it was a few minutes to 7 p.m. and, having the benefit of the professor's attention, solicited his help in securing my own membership in the Gray-Headed League. "You know everyone in the bridge world, couldn't you intercede on my behalf? I certainly could use the money."

He said nothing, but grabbed his cap and coat and strode out the door. I followed and we walked in silence to the R—- Bridge Club. We entered, and Silver whispered something to the proprietor who nodded and pointed to a group of men sitting round a table nearby. Silver addressed them in a low, but firm voice.

"Gentlemen, you have been guilty of a cruel fraud, perpetrated on an unsuspecting bridge player. I am speaking of course, of MacDonald Bird; a more decent man never breathed, and he's certainly a far better person than any of you despicable rogues. Incidentally, I see there are only five conspirators here; where is the sixth?"

Their response to this astonishing diatribe was to call over a sixth man who had been buying an entry for the evening duplicate.

"I shall not waste my breath expressing my contempt for your behaviour but merely content myself with observing that Bird would have legal recourse to your bank accounts should he ever discover your humiliating fraud. I shall keep silent if you abide by the following conditions. You will maintain the offices of the Gray-Headed League until Bird finds a regular job. You will cut back his hours to three evenings a week. And, finally, you will, each of you in turn, play bridge with him once a week for a year. In addition you will play sectional team games with him, in alternating platoons of three, for the same period of time. Agreed?"

The six looked sheepishly at one another; finally, one of them spoke. "We never meant him any harm. It's just that he's such an erratic bridge player that we can't stand him as a partner and he's such a nice guy, we can't bear to refuse him — and we did want to help him out financially until he finds work."

"That last," thundered Silver, "is the only mitigating factor in this sorry affair. For that reason alone I shall keep your secret. Your problem is common in the bridge world and you will have to learn how to deal with it."

The evening duplicate was about to begin and I suggested to Silver that we might as well stay and play .

"No," he replied; then, turning to the conspirators, he said "See how easy it is?"

"The case was an interesting one," said Professor Silver later that evening, settling into his favourite chair and picking up his well-thumbed copy of *Famous Whist Hands of the Nineteenth Century*, "Because it serves to show how simple the explanation may be of an affair which at first sight seems almost incomprehensible."

"How in the world did you know there was a conspiracy to keep Bird away from bridge? Had he said something significant before I arrived?" I asked.

"My dear Cardinal, the second I saw the advertisement I knew that something was amiss. Is it conceivable that an organization should exist for the sole purpose of dispensing money to gray-haired bridge players and that you, not to mention a million other financially-challenged denizens of the bridge clubs, would not have heard of it? Had Bird been married, I would have suspected a mere vulgar intrigue. Once that possibility was eliminated, it became perfectly obvious that the only possible object of this preposterous scheme was to keep him away from duplicate games and tournaments; that much was clear from the designated hours of employment. The advertisement itself was probably brought to his attention by one of the conspirators. The number of conspirators was easy to infer from the $600 a week salary. And by the way, I have myself played with Bird, and I must confess, I would gladly pay a hundred dollars to avoid repeating the experience."

"But surely, Professor, you were too harsh on the conspirators," I responded. "Is not the unfortunate Bird the author of his own misfortune? Are we not all doomed continually to deflect importuning acolytes who rob us of precious table time? It seems to me that their little stratagem at once saved their sanity and Bird's self-respect. Where could the wrong in that be?"

"Author of his own misfortune, you say!" he bellowed. "And of what, pray tell, is he guilty? He flatters those who find his attentions so burdensome, and he comes out to every tournament in the district, supporting the game in the only meaningful way — with his time and money. May I point out to you that master points are given out in direct proportion to the number of tables in play? How many master points would you win if the Birds of this world stayed at home?"

"I must confess I never thought of it in those terms. But surely," I ventured timidly, "there is a difference between 'playing with' and 'partnering'?"

"Of course there is, but we can't just take from bridge, we must give something back. Could not each of those six self-styled experts have played with Bird twice a year, giving him a thrilling session once a month with little inconvenience to themselves?"

"But Professor, you never play with people you consider lesser in ability than yourself. I have been asking you for a game for months, but you never even bother to invent an excuse, you just refuse me."

" 'Let him who is without sin cast the first stone', is that what you are saying, Cardinal? Well, for your information, I play once a year with an old friend of mine — actually, on the Saturday following Good Friday, and I sincerely hope the symbolism continues to elude him. Why, you ask? Because once a year he catches a glimpse of what he could be if he stopped frittering away his time with his career and family. You, however, could never hope to attain my level of proficiency and a game with me would only plunge you into the depths of despair.

"I don't mean to be unkind," he continued, "but as Doctor Johnson pointed out 'the benefits of kindness can only be bestowed as others are capable to receive' and you, my dear Cardinal, are only a simple squeeze above Bird.

"You do understand, don't you?"

HUNTING THE GREAT WHITE WHALE

Call me Cardinal. Some years ago — never mind how long precisely — having little or no money in my wallet, I took up lodgings with Professor Silver and devoted my life to bridge. At the outset of my career, money was in short supply and many a time I turned to him for a loan, or more frequently, a deferment for that month's rent. He never refused, nor would he suffer any mention of his previous kindnesses when I later attempted to fulfill my pecuniary obligations. So when he embarked upon his great quest, I was obliged to accompany him.

Old age is always wakeful; as if, the longer linked with life, the less man wants to do with aught that looks like death. Among bridge players, too, it is the graybeards that most often leave their beds to visit the cool air of night. At the time of which I write, Professor Silver of late had become alomst entirely nocturnal, pacing the length of our sitting room for hours, muttering in subdued tones.

One night I awakened and found him as he paced his rounds, upon carpets so familiar to his tread that they were all over dented with the peculiar mark of his walk. As I fixed my gaze on his ribbed and dented brow, I saw still stranger footprints — the footprints of his one unsleeping, ever-pacing thought. And so full of his thought was Professor Silver, that at every turn that he made, now at the wall and now at the television set, you could almost see that thought turn in him as he turned, and pace in him as he paced; so completely possessing him, that it all but seemed to be driving him mad.

"Cardinal," he moaned, "you must help me find the Great

White Whale. I hate him, he taunts me in my dreams, he fills my every waking hour with a remorse that embitters my life. I am obsessed with the notion that I shall die without having my revenge upon him. Thirty years I have pursued him relentlessly and on each encounter he has bested me. I must find him before it is too late, as already I can sense my abilities diminishing. Still, while much has been taken, much abides; I can still beat him, if you will help."

"Who is the Great White Whale?" I asked, although I already divined that this must be some bridge opponent of singular ability.

"I first encountered him at the 1954 Spring Nationals. I was just beginning to establish my reputation with the leading players of the day, and you know, Cardinal, how important is the esteem of one's peers to an ambitious young bridge player. It was the first round of the Vanderbilt teams and I was playing with Helen Sobel, our partners being Charles Goren and John Gerber. Not a great team, but the best the partnership desk could arrange for me at the last minute.

"I had complained of our being seeded only fifth, but the director informed me that although I was Captain, the committee had felt that the team as a whole did not merit a higher seed. Of course we were playing a team that was seeded below 100, four amateurs who lived at the bottom of the tournament food-chain. I picked up the first hand, and as dealer, white against red, I held:

♠ 6 5　♡ 4 3 2　♢ 3 2　♣ 9 8 5 4 3 2

"Perhaps, subliminally, I was goaded by the shoals of kibitzers that surrounded my table. I was, after all, still very young, so I decided to cast my net in search of some early IMPs. Eschewing the obvious pre-emptive club bid, I opened with a strong notrump. LHO bid a natural 3♡ and Mrs. Sobel bid 4♣, which was clearly ace-asking, and which I intended to pass!

"Alas, RHO doubled and I pondered the various options available to me, all of them equally unappetizing. A pass would clearly be forcing under the circumstances, a redouble an invitation to disaster, and any suit call would guarantee the appropriate number of aces. What would you bid, Cardinal?"

I mumbled something inaudible, as I saw no way of extricating the great man from his self-inflicted predicament.

"I, of course, found the expert bid: 5♣. LHO passed, to my

great relief, but my partner disappointed me by bidding an ill-considered 6NT, which was promptly doubled and became the final contract. The opening lead was a small heart and the dummy appeared:

HELEN SOBEL

♠ J 10 3 2
♡ K J
♢ K Q 4
♣ A K J 6

YOUNG SILVER

♠ 6 5
♡ 4 3 2
♢ 3 2
♣ 9 8 5 4 3 2

"I called for the ♡J, certain that even a rank amateur would not underlead an ace against a doubled slam, and RHO took the trick with the queen. Back came a low spade, won by the queen on my left. The ♡A was played as RHO showed out! Five more hearts followed, each one placed slowly and deliberately upon the table as dummy fell victim to an inexorable progressive squeeze.

I discarded three clubs and a small diamond from the dummy but the last heart presented me with the choice of unguarding the spade suit or discarding either the king or queen of diamonds or the club ace. Hoping for a blockage in spades, I grimly kept the honours and shed a small spade. Back came a another spade and RHO cashed the ace, king, and nine in that suit while LHO discarded a diamond.

Dummy followed to the first two spades, but was squeezed again on the third. If I threw the club ace, East could score the queen, while if I threw a diamond, West would take the last two tricks with the ace and jack of diamonds. There had been no escape after my initial mis-guess of the heart position:

HELEN SOBEL
♠ J 10 3 2
♡ K J
♢ K Q 4
♣ A K J 6

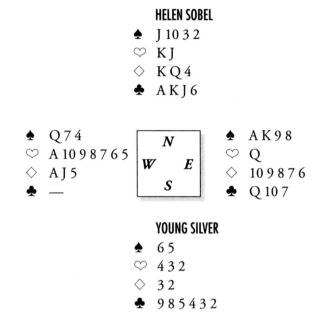

♠ Q 7 4
♡ A 10 9 8 7 6 5
♢ A J 5
♣ —

♠ A K 9 8
♡ Q
♢ 10 9 8 7 6
♣ Q 10 7

YOUNG SILVER
♠ 6 5
♡ 4 3 2
♢ 3 2
♣ 9 8 5 4 3 2

"Twelve down?" enquired LHO of Mrs. Sobel. "What's that, 2300?"

And at that point, he sounded. There is no other word for it, Cardinal — LHO sounded. A high-pitched whine erupted from deep within him, his face turned red and he shrieked "Twelve down!" and he laughed. He was a huge man, with cheeks like pillows and long blonde hair which fell in his eyes as he collapsed in paroxysms of laughter.

"Twelve down doubled!" he bellowed, as his partner started to laugh too. "Could've taken three tricks at least, heh, heh, heh, but you lost all thirteen!" Roars of laughter billowed up from the kibitzers and crashed upon my head like the surf crushing a pebble against a rocky shore. Even my partner laughed. It seemed as though the entire membership of the ACBL was laughing as I staggered to my feet and fled from the table followed by the peals of mirth emanating from my table. I did not return.

"I spent my six months tournament suspension researching my ribald opponent. His name was Grant Weatherby Wilson, a high school

---

teacher from Bedford, Massachusetts. He was known to fellow denizens of the bridge depths as the Great White Whale because of his girth and pallid colouring. GWW played only once or twice a year, always with his brother, Frank 'The Kipper' Wilson. They had a combined master point holding of 1.5, earned at a steady pace of 0.25 a year.

"I did not see either of them again for several years. It was a Spring Nationals in the middle 60's, when young Hambly and I were on our way to our first win in a prestigious Open Pairs event. We were sailing along collecting tops at a dizzying pace until late in the evening I picked up:

♠ 10 6 4   ♡ K Q 10 9 2   ◇ A 5 3   ♣ K 6

Hambly opened the bidding with a diamond and we quickly and efficiently bid our way into the optimum matchpoint contract, 3NT. As declarer, I awaited the opening lead. A hush fell over the gathered throng of kibitzers and then I heard it, a high pitched giggle emanating from LHO. Up to this moment, as is my wont, I had not bothered to look at my opponents or their convention cards. But now I slowly turned to my left and found myself staring into the piscine eyes of the Great White Whale. He suppressed another giggle and led the ♠J.

"Cardinal, it was the only lead to beat the contract!"

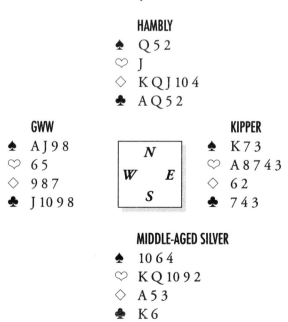

HAMBLY

♠ Q 5 2
♡ J
◇ K Q J 10 4
♣ A Q 5 2

GWW
♠ A J 9 8
♡ 6 5
◇ 9 8 7
♣ J 10 9 8

KIPPER
♠ K 7 3
♡ A 8 7 4 3
◇ 6 2
♣ 7 4 3

MIDDLE-AGED SILVER

♠ 10 6 4
♡ K Q 10 9 2
◇ A 5 3
♣ K 6

"On the lead of any suit but spades, or the lead of any spade other than the jack, the contract is cold. On the natural club lead, chosen by the majority of defenders, South wins and drives out the ace of hearts. Now the defence has to be alert and cash their two top spades, else declarer will make six notrumps. Every declarer in the field made overtricks in a three notrumps contract. Except me.

"A small spade lead I could have ducked, but you will see, of course, Cardinal, that after the ♠J lead I was doomed. At the table, I played low hoping that GWW had led from four or five to the ♠J10. But the jack held the trick, and they continued with a low spade to the king, two more spades and the heart ace for one down. Had I put up the spade queen at trick one, East would have won the king and returned a spade through my ten for the same result. On a 51 top, the complete zero robbed us of the win; indeed, it knocked us out of the top twenty. We never came close to winning anything again.

"And so it continued. For years that man has haunted me. You know how infrequently I play, yet every time I am leading in an event, he surfaces and drags me down into the lower depths. In thirty years, I have never won an IMP nor taken a matchpoint from him. He now has 7.4 registered masterpoints, each extracted, it seems, a fraction at a time, from me. I'm sorry Cardinal, I cannot continue."

And he buried his head in his hands, as I muttered what inadequate words of support and consolation I could muster to relieve my friend's distress.

Some little time after this conversation, during the recent Toronto Nationals, I had been knocked out of the first round of the Spingold and had remained to kibitz the survivors. Naturally I headed immediately to Professor Silver's table where, fighting my way through the crush of onlookers, I secured a vantage point directly behind him from which I could see all the hands. Professor Silver was playing with Bruce Gowdy, a volatile combination of personalities which promised good entertainment coupled with excellent bridge. The professor, however. seemed uncharacteristically subdued and was certainly not bidding to thin games with his customary élan. This puzzled me until I noticed the man sitting to his left. A shock of recognition passed over me; this could only be the Great White Whale! It was at that moment that Silver was dealt a hand that has since become famous.

♠ Q 10 9 8 7 6 5 4 3   ♡ —   ◇ A 8   ♣ 9 6

The Kipper (for I had deduced that it must be he) on Silver's right was dealer, and opened a strong notrump. I gazed in fascination at the hand and tried to discover the master bid. How many spades would the vulnerable Professor Silver bid? The opponents could easily be on for a game, indeed, a vulnerable slam might be there for the bidding. My choice was 4♠, but knowing Professor Silver's tactical genius, I did not rule out a heart preempt on his void, or bidding diamonds at some level to direct Gowdy to the best lead. After all, holding the spade suit, one could always correct later.

But even I, knowing him as well as I did, could not anticipate what he actually did. He passed. He passed quickly, smoothly, and in perfect tempo. The great white one bid 2◇. This was alerted, and upon Mr. Gowdy's inquiry, identified as forcing Stayman. Gowdy passed and East jumped to 3♡. Everyone knew this was a slam try in an auction that was already forced to game, so it now came as no surprise to me when the professor elected to pass once again.

It was a surprise, however, when 3♡ was passed out — quickly by GWW, and, very slowly, by Bruce Gowdy. A low spade was led, West tabled the dummy and began to giggle.

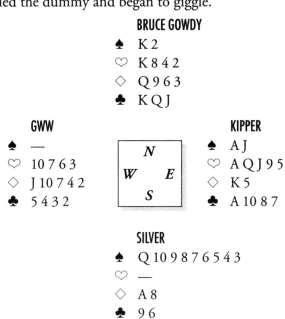

BRUCE GOWDY
♠ K 2
♡ K 8 4 2
◇ Q 9 6 3
♣ K Q J

GWW
♠ —
♡ 10 7 6 3
◇ J 10 7 4 2
♣ 5 4 3 2

N
W   E
S

KIPPER
♠ A J
♡ A Q J 9 5
◇ K 5
♣ A 10 8 7

SILVER
♠ Q 10 9 8 7 6 5 4 3
♡ —
◇ A 8
♣ 9 6

Declarer made exactly three hearts, despite the bad trump break, losing a heart, two clubs, and only one diamond when he guessed the position of the ace. Professor Silver had managed to keep his composure and tried to throw the hand in quickly but his nemesis was having none of that. He pointed out that North-South had both spades and points and surely they could make something? Mr. Gowdy, upon discovering his partner's distribution, rose to his feet and was about unleash his wrath upon the hapless Silver when the GWW started to laugh.

"I'm sorry, guys," he giggled. "I forgot we were playing two-way Stayman. I bid 2◇ to play, and just passed in a panic when my partner bid hearts. I didn't mean to fool anybody. But I sure never dreamed I could shut out a nine-card spade suit just by bidding Stayman." And he laughed again.

And then Bruce Gowdy started to laugh. "I suppose," he chuckled, "you were waiting for the right moment to bid your nine-bagger. And you'll still be waiting tomorrow!"

The kibitzers joined in his mirth, and so did the caddies and players at nearby tables as the story spread. It seemed as though the entire Royal York Hotel was laughing, with the exception of Professor Silver who just sat, staring at the floor. Finally, he rose and, glancing neither to the left nor the right, strode out into the wintry night. I struggled through the throng and followed as quickly as I could.

The fresh tracks in the snow led me South, down York Street towards the lake, and I hastened my steps in a vain effort to catch up to him before he reached the shore. I followed to the water's edge but found only a crumpled convention card. Nothing else was visible except the cold black water which rolled up against the ferry docks. Of my old friend and mentor, there was no sign at all.....

HEARTS OF DARKNESS

I don't want to bother you much with what happened to me personally, just for you to understand how I went to that place where I met Kurtz. It was in the farthest reaches of the tournament world and was in some ways the turning point of my career.

Many months had passed since Silver's disappearance. I had just then returned to Toronto after a regular dose of the tournament trail — New York, Los Angeles, Dallas — and I was loafing about, playing afternoon duplicates. I was soon running out of money so I began to look around for paid games. Bridge had once again ceased for me to be an avocation to dream gloriously over and instead become a vocation upon which I depended for sustenance. But clients proved to be impossible to obtain. I blamed the hard times, but a frank evaluation soon revealed how dependent I had been on referrals from Professor Silver for my livelihood. He, of course was gone, and I was forced to contemplate the bleak prospect of seeking ordinary employment.

Then I got the letter. It was from Mia Culpa, a bridge enthusiast living in the depths of New England. She had recently come into a substantial inheritance, taken early retirement, and was ready to embark on a quest for master points. She offered a substantial stipend for a six month's tour of the local tournament trail — all expenses paid. There was one codicil: the arrangement would be terminated if a certain Mr. Kurtz were to become available as her partner. I accepted by return mail, pawned my laptop, and boarded the bus for Massachusetts.

I had no difficulty in finding the bridge club when I arrived:

it was in the local hotel and everybody I met was going to the afternoon game. It was on a narrow and deserted street in deep shadow, innumerable windows with Venetian blinds, a dead silence, grass sprouting between the stones, imposing carriage archways right and left, immense double doors standing ponderously ajar. I slipped through one of these cracks, went up a swept and ungarnished staircase and opened the first door I came to. Two women, one young and the other old, sat on straw-bottomed chairs, reading tattered back copies of *Canadian Master Point* almost as if they understood them. One of them was my client.

I went to work that very weekend. A local regional was within a few hours drive and we arrived, breathlessly, in time for the Open Pairs. My task was, by some professional alchemy, to convert my partner's inept bidding and play into gold points. The first hand was a portent of things to come. I held:

♠ Q 5 3   ♡ K 10 9 8   ◇ K 6 3   ♣ A Q 2

Mia dealt and opened 1♠, RHO passed, and I bid the obvious forcing 3♠. LHO overcalled 4◇, and Mia bid 4♠ which became the final contract. The ◇Q arrived on the table and we quickly went two down, vulnerable.

MIA
♠ A K 8 7 2
♡ A J 6
◇ 8 7
♣ 7 6 4

♠ 10		♠ J 9 6 4
♡ 7 4 3 2	N	♡ Q 5
◇ A J 10 9 5 4	W E	◇ Q 2
♣ 5 3	S	♣ K J 10 9 8

CARDINAL
♠ Q 5 3
♡ K 10 9 8
◇ K 6 3
♣ A Q 2

Mia covered the ♢Q with the king; West won the trick with the ace and then attempted to cash two more diamonds. Mia thought, thought, and thought some more, finally ruffing low as East discarded. Cashing the queen, ace, and king of trumps revealed to everyone but Mia that there was an inescapable trump loser. Mia finessed dummy's ♣Q, cashed the ♡K and took the heart finesse, her jack losing to the queen. East now played the ♠J extracting Mia's last trump, and returned a club to the ace. With the heart suit irretrievably blocked, she could come to only one more trick.

"Oh dear," Mia said, "minus 200 is always a bottom, isn't it? I'm sorry, it's all my fault. I'll do better."

She was correct in her analysis, but wrong in her prediction: that disaster turned out to be one of our bettter boards of the afternoon. Later, I watched helplessly while she mangled the dummy in a cold three no trumps contract. After winning the opening lead (her ninth trick) she ignored dummy's solid suit and side ace and attempted to set up winners in her own hand. Later, instead of claiming her contract, she endplayed RHO so that our amazed opponents could cash their seven winners. The six months stretching ahead of me suddenly seemed longer than eternity.

Board #1 came up again in conversation between sessions. Everyone at our dinner table had been plus or minus 100, depending on whether they had played or defended four spades. Everyone, that is, but us, our opponents, and one other gentleman: he had been minus 1430. Perplexed, I asked him to explain.

"Well, I had the diamond hand. North opened 1♠, my partner passed, and South bid 2♡. I overcalled 3♢, North bid 3♡ and South checked for aces and raised himself to six. I figured that the only chance to beat it was a diamond ruff, so I made the unfortunate lead of ace and another diamond. It was all over."

"What do you mean? With the spades not splitting, declarer still has to lose a club."

"Not this declarer. He actually claimed after winning the ♢K, although he refused to explain his line of play, saying it was too obvious to discuss. We protested, and called the director, and eventually he condescended to play the hand out."

"What was his line of play?"

```
              ♠  A K 8 7 2
              ♡  A J 6
              ◇  8 7
              ♣  7 6 4

♠  10                          ♠  J 9 6 4
♡  7 4 3 2      ┌─────────┐    ♡  Q 5
◇  A J 10 9 5 4 │    N    │    ◇  Q 2
♣  5 3          │ W     E │    ♣  K J 10 9 8
                │    S    │
                └─────────┘
              KURTZ
              ♠  Q 5 3
              ♡  K 10 9 8
              ◇  K 6 3
              ♣  A Q 2
```

"After winning the ◇K, he ruffed his last diamond with dummy's
♡A as my partner shed a club. He then played dummy's ♡J, winning
his king when my partner covered with the queen. As my remaining
trumps were drawn, my poor partner was squeezed in the black suits. His
only hope was that I had the ♣Q so he held on to four spades while re-
ducing his club holding to the doubleton king, jack. Declarer didn't even
bother to test the spade suit, but crossed over to dummy's queen and took
the club finesse, cashed his two high spades and the ♣A, and took his
twelfth trick with the ♣2! Declarer's only comment was 'a classic Gowdy
ending', whatever that means."

"You must have been playing against Kurtz," said Mia.

Several agreed, and they all began to talk about Kurtz and his ob-
session with the heart suit. Kurtz had made four hearts redoubled on a
three-three fit; Kurtz had doubled a grand slam for a heart lead; Kurtz
had, in fact, bid or overcalled hearts on nearly every hand that he held.
Yet he made impossible hands, he defeated iron-clad contracts, and he
never discussed his bids or plays, even with his partners.

"Don't you talk with Mr. Kurtz when you play with him?" I
asked Mia.

"You don't talk with Mr. Kurtz, you take notes. I don't even think he eats or sleeps. He just plays bridge and analyzes bridge hands. I asked him to join us for dinner tonight, but he just grunted and sat down in the hotel lobby to read a book called *Endplays* by some Frenchman called de Sade."

With a suspicion that was rapidly hardening to certainty, I rose from the table and retraced my steps to the hotel. Peering around the empty lobby, I saw a large armchair facing the wall, and I could see the back of a grizzled head bent over a yellow-covered book as I approached. I coughed discreetly, but the chair's occupant took no notice of me nor of my increasingly overt intrusions on his privacy. Finally, I took him by the arm, shook him, and said, "Professor Silver, I presume?"

For it was he. As a glimmering of recognition passed over his face, I could not help but notice how much he had changed physically since I last saw him. He was much aged, but I was struck by the fire of his eyes and the composed languor of his expression. I was even further surprised when he spoke, for after our initial exclamations of good fellowship and reunion, Professor Silver began to discourse! His voice rang deep as he revealed the wastes of his weary brain, haunted by shadowy images — images of Grant Weatherby Wilson, of Bruce Gowdy, of partners now long departed. His solitary meditations had produced new insights into the game, and he was now convinced of the supremacy of the heart suit above all else. But his diabolic hatred for the Great White Whale fought above all for the possession of his soul as I listened in horror.

"Cardinal, with what opportune timing you rejoin me in this hour! I am closing in on the Great White Whale. For months I have been tracking him, studying his habits, planning my revenge. Of late, he plays only in novice games in an attempt to avoid me, but I have assumed the identity of a retired mathematician from Austria, and it is assumed by all that I have no master points! Tomorrow, he plays in the Severely Restricted Open Pairs. We shall conceal your identity and play the same event, and when he surfaces, I shall wreak my revenge upon him. You see, I know how to beat him — the heart suit is the key, Cardinal! That's how we shall get him, my old friend, with the heart suit!"

The ties of friendshiop are strong, and the next day I found myself playing in the swamp, a consolation game for those players who had failed to qualify for the second session of a playthrough event. Although we had made several sightings, we had yet to accost Wilson himself. As we progressed silently from table to table, I asked myself what it all meant. People sat in the semi-darkness holding small pieces of plastic in their hands, like a lot of pilgrims bewitched by the promise of paradise. The phrase 'master point' rang in the air, was whispered, was sighed. You would think they were praying to it. I was aroused from my lethargy when Grant Weatherby Wilson smiled as we sat down at his table. Judgment day had arrived!

He glanced suspiciously at us and looked at my card, but upon seeing the names Melville and Kurtz, picked up his hand and studied it. I heard GWW bid 1♠ on my left and I looked up anxiously at Professor Silver, but he seemingly took no offence at this blasphemous intrusion into his auction and calmly bid 2♡. The Kipper, on my right, bid 2♠ (a constructive raise) and I looked at my hand:

♠ 9 3   ♡ K Q 2   ◇ 8 7 2   ♣ A 8 7 6 2

I preempted with 4♡, which was followed instantly by 4♠ from GWW. Professor Silver doubled this audacity, which was in turn, redoubled by the large, pallid one. My partner led the ♣Q, the dummy appeared, and I prayed for divine guidance as declarer called for a low club from dummy.

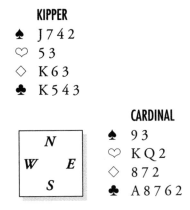

Professor Silver's career path is paved with the tombstones of partners who failed to make intelligent decisions at crucial moments. I overtook the ♣Q with the ace and led the eight back. GWW followed and the professor ruffed. He returned the ♡9 and I won the trick, dummy and declarer both playing low. I agonized over cashing another heart before returning a club, but I could visualize the post mortem.

"Surely, Cardinal, if we could take two heart tricks, I would have cashed one and then put you in to give me another ruff?"

I returned another club, the only play to beat the hand.

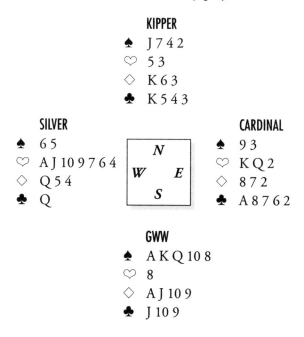

KIPPER
♠ J 7 4 2
♡ 5 3
♢ K 6 3
♣ K 5 4 3

SILVER
♠ 6 5
♡ A J 10 9 7 6 4
♢ Q 5 4
♣ Q

CARDINAL
♠ 9 3
♡ K Q 2
♢ 8 7 2
♣ A 8 7 6 2

GWW
♠ A K Q 10 8
♡ 8
♢ A J 10 9
♣ J 10 9

Plus four hundred, a clear top even this den of ineptitude. I stole a glance at Professor Silver. Three decades seemed to have been lifted from his shoulders. He sat up straight in his chair and eagerly picked up the next hand. He glanced at it and passed, as did the Kipper. I had a more than useful hand:

♠ A 9 2 ♡ K J ♢ A Q 9 7 ♣ Q J 10 2

Arguing that his methods allowed us the more easily to reach all potential heart fits, the professor had prevailed upon me to play weak no trumps. Partnership style required me to open the bidding with my lowest suit, so I bid 1♣. Wilson, never one to be intimidated, over-called 1♡, which was followed by two passes. I was systemically bound to reopen with a double, so I uttered that ominous word. GWW passed, Professor Silver passed, RHO passed, and I looked about for the nearest exit.

The opening lead was the ♡2!

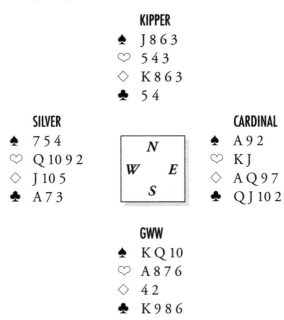

KIPPER
♠ J 8 6 3
♡ 5 4 3
◇ K 8 6 3
♣ 5 4

SILVER
♠ 7 5 4
♡ Q 10 9 2
◇ J 10 5
♣ A 7 3

CARDINAL
♠ A 9 2
♡ K J
◇ A Q 9 7
♣ Q J 10 2

GWW
♠ K Q 10
♡ A 8 7 6
◇ 4 2
♣ K 9 8 6

The defence was cruel. Wilson won my ♡K and banged down the ♠K, which I took with my ace. I now played the ♡J which was overtaken by the professor, who drew declarer's trumps as I shed my remaining spades. The ◇J was now put on the table, pinning dummy's king! I ran four rounds of diamonds and switched to the ♣Q: declarer put up the ♡K and we took the last three tricks — fourteen hundred! I breathed a silent thanks to the ghoulie gods and looked around. The Greatly Girthed Wilson was laughing uproariously, and Professor Silver joined in as I watched, amazed.

"Boy, did you guys ever teach me a lesson," GWW giggled. "I'll never overcall a four-card suit again — at least, not against you two. What a score! Oh well, it's only a game. If you're not having fun, why bother playing?"

Professor Silver smiled at him, fondly I thought, and said nothing. The director called the round and we rose to go to the next table. GWW bade us a friendly good-bye as we moved on.

During the long drive back to Toronto, Silver was atypically quiet. Usually as I drove, he would regale me with hoary anecdotes of famous matches between the legendary heroes of the Golden Age of Bridge, which he identified as the years between his thirtieth and sixtieth birthdays. After about four hours he spoke.

"You see, Cardinal, we have lost the spirit of the game. You are obsessed with winning and I with the technical minutiae of the hands. We have both lost sight of the prime imperative, to enjoy ourselves. The Great White Whale is more of a bridge player than you or I will ever be: he plays for the sport. Think how much more pleasant bridge competitions would be if everyone were as friendly and sportsmanlike as the brothers Wilson.

"By the way, I have invited them to play in the next Spingold with us. I assume that's all right with you?"

"Of course, Professor. We'll have a whale of a time."

FREE BIRD SEED

Claude is my bridge partner and we're getting pretty good. We beat up all the nerds in the common-room bridge games and we win the campus bridge club duplicate every Tuesday night (well, most weeks). Claude's real scene is computer programming but he likes bridge because 'it's better than real life'. If Claude were a *Jeopardy!* contestant, his seven dream categories would be:

    * Intel assembly language
    * Meals made from combinations of Frito-Lay flavours
    * Frequent and anonymous sex
    * Sega Genesis gaming addiction
    * C++
    * Psychotically ambitious parents
    * Double-dummy bridge problems

Claude's really old — 23 — but he's cool. We're both seniors at Mohican College majoring in beer-drinking and partying. My name's Jim Hawkins and I hate Professor Silver.

Hate is probably too mild a word for it, more likely, DESPISE, LOATHE, ABHOR, DETEST, take your pick. Ever since I bulled my way through his Bridge 101 night-school class I've dreamed of ways of flaming that ancient sage-on-the-stage. His bridge-o-centric world view is fifty years out of date and his unreadable book *Bridge the Silver Way*, the required text naturally, should have been illuminated by monks on parchment instead of being printed on paper. His theories are moronic, especially 'The Supremacy of the Heart Suit' or his 'Law of Precise Provocation' and he flunks anyone who dares disagree with him. If Professor Silver were a *Jeopardy!* contestant, his seven dream categories would be:

* Bitterness
* Arcane and idiotic bidding theories
* The art and science of putting down students
* More bitterness
* Frequent and losing bridge
* The bridge scene 1928-1956
* Psychotic loser bridge partners

BRING ME THE HEAD OF PROFESSOR SILVER!

More details about my vendetta — The Quest for Silver

Because he has no interest except bridge, I am determined to humiliate him publicly, at the bridge table. From midnight to dawn I am on-line with his ex-students on alt.getsilver.S+M.com, an Internet discussion group dedicated to revenge fantasies. One of our 4000+ members has hacked Doom® so that all the monsters morph into Professor Silver after you kill them. INTERESTING SOCIOLOGICAL ABNORMALITY — Doom® Silver is the only computer game that has more female players than males, go figure! The girls participate in the discussions and are very imaginative.

THROW YOUR CARDS ON THE TABLE AND HAND OVER ALL YOUR MATCHPOINTS — RESISTANCE IS FUTILE!

At last — we've finally arrived at Professor Silver's table. I'm gonna get ya, sucka!

"Good evening, professor," I say as pleasantly as I can manage. "By the way, why did you give me a 'D' in Bridge 101?"

"Because I like you," he says with a sneer. "Wright, these boys are spade bidders, that should tell you everything you need to know about their bridge abilities."

What a geek that Wright Cardinal is. That Groucho mustache keeps bobbing up and down as he chews, hopefully, gum. How can he play with that bad-tempered cryptofascist? If Cardinal were a TV program, he'd be "You Bet Your Life" — make the wrong bid and a bird descends and whacks you over the head. Cardinal is opening the bidding with a pass, I'd better look at my hand.

♠ A 8 7 3 2 ♡ K 4 ◇ K Q 5 3 ♣ 6 2

I bid one spade, Silver passes and Claude bids two spades (inverted major raises, Silver's fault of course). I rebid three diamonds, and Claude's four spades ends the bidding. Silver leads the jack of clubs and the dummy appears.

CLAUDE		JIM
♠ Q 10 9	N	♠ A 8 7 3 2
♡ A 5 3	W E	♡ K 4
◇ A 6	S	◇ K Q 5 3
♣ Q 9 5 4		♣ 6 2

I duck the jack and cover the ten of clubs on the next trick, so now Cardinal is in. He returns a heart, which I win in dummy. First I have to deal with my diamond loser, so I play off the ace and king, and ruff the third round in the dummy. Wright Cardinal OVERRUFFS WITH THE KING! Then he returns a heart, not even trying for a trump promotion with another club. The whole hand is obvious now; how can I phrase my claim so best to annoy Professor Silver? I win the heart, and lead a spade, to which the professor follows low.

"Win that with the ten," I say to Claude as Professor Silver laughs. "What's so funny? Oh no! You had the spade jack too, Mr. Cardinal?"

"And my poor fool is hanged," sneers Professor Silver.

"Geekspeak? What's he talking about?" asks Claude.

FREE BIRD SEED (FBS)

"Permit me to translate," says Professor Silver. "Remember the old 'Roadrunner' cartoons? The roadrunner was incapable of passing a 'Free Bird Seed' sign. Uncatchable while moving, he'd put himself in danger by stopping and pecking at the pile of seed, never asking himself who painted the sign. You likely had a diamond loser on the auction, and if my partner either overruffed with the jack, or attempted to give me a trump promotion, you could hardly fail to take the wining line of play. But when Cardinal played the king of spades from his KJ doubleton, you assumed I had the spade jack and stopped running to peck at your imaginary game."

I pick up the next hand:

♠ J 9 6 5   ♡ K J 9 8 5   ◇ 9   ♣ 10 7 3

Professor Silver opens the bidding with one heart (what else?) and Claude preempts with three diamonds. Cardinal bids three spades, I pass and Professor Silver bids four hearts. Claude passes and Cardinal raises Professor Silver to six hearts. Gotcha Professor! "I DOUBLE"

Everyone passes and Claude leads a small spade, dummy's first bid suit. Cardinal puts the dummy on the table.

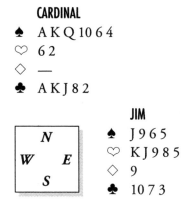

CARDINAL
♠   A K Q 10 6 4
♡   6 2
◇   —
♣   A K J 8 2

JIM
♠   J 9 6 5
♡   K J 9 8 5
◇   9
♣   10 7 3

Winning the ♣A, Professor Silver calls for dummy's deuce of hearts, I play my five and declarer wins the trick with the seven as Claude discards a small diamond! He then ruffs a diamond, cashing two more spade honours while throwing diamonds from his hand. Now he ruffs my jack of spades and then successfully finesses dummy's jack of clubs bringing me and the dummy down to:

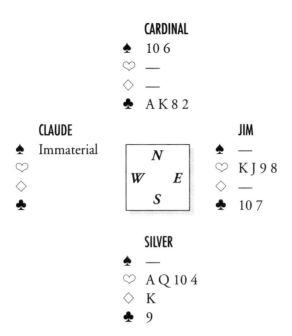

CARDINAL
- ♠ 10 6
- ♡ —
- ◇ —
- ♣ A K 8 2

CLAUDE
- ♠ Immaterial
- ♡
- ◇
- ♣

JIM
- ♠ —
- ♡ K J 9 8
- ◇ —
- ♣ 10 7

SILVER
- ♠ —
- ♡ A Q 10 4
- ◇ K
- ♣ 9

Professor Silver now cashes the ♣AK, and leads a third club which I ruff with the eight. He overruffs with the ten and leads out a small trump which I have to win with my nine. I am endplayed, and have to lead from my ♡K J into his AQ.

"FBS!" crows Professor Silver. "If you had split your heart honours at trick two I couldn't make the hand, but you were too busy thinking up sarcastic witticisms to pay attention, weren't you? Didn't you think that you would disclose the bad trump split if you doubled? And was it necessary to double on a hand where any plus score will give you a top board?"

WOULDN'T THE WORLD BE A BETTER PLACE IF IT WERE RUN BY THE TELEPHONE COMPANY?

Then I could take out my cellular phone, dial 1-800-KILL-PROF and hear:

To drain Professor Silver's bodily fluids....Press 1.
To have Professor Silver's still-beating heart thrown into a shark-infested hot tub....Press 2.
If you have a rotary phone...stay on the line and he will be disembowelled as soon as one of our representatives is free.

"Your bid, Jim."

I look at my hand:

♠ Q 7 6 2   ♡ 8 6 5   ◇ 9 7   ♣ Q 7 6 3

I pass. Professor Silver bids one heart and Claude overcalls with 3◇. Cardinal raises to 3♡ which I pass, and the Professor carries on to 4♡. Claude leads the ♠J and we all admire the dummy.

CARDINAL
♠ K 5 3
♡ Q 4 3
◇ 10 6 2
♣ A 5 4 2

JIM

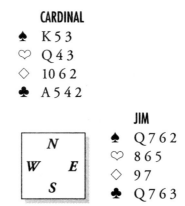

♠ Q 7 6 2
♡ 8 6 5
◇ 9 7
♣ Q 7 6 3

Professor Silver looks at the ♠J and then plays low from the dummy as I follow, and wins the ace in hand. Now he plays the ace and king of trumps, Claude following to both, and then he puts the ♣J on the table. Claude covers it with the king, declarer wins the ace and quickly returns a low club from the dummy.

I start to play the ♣Q, but I hesitate. "What if," I say to myself, "Claude started with a doubleton K10"? I would compress our two club tricks if I rose with my queen and smothered his now singleton 10. Even worse, Professor Silver might be down to J 9 and have to guess which one to play. I play low and Professor Silver wins the ten as Claude drops the nine.

He crosses to dummy's ♠K, ruffs its last spade and throws me in with a club. But he has forgotten to draw my last trump, big mistake Professor. I lead the ◇9 through anticipating a ruff. Professor Silver plays low, Claude wins the jack....and goes into a trance. Finally he returns a low diamond which Professor Silver wins with the queen. He then plays a heart to the queen and claims five.

"Three mistakes in one round Jim?" sneers Professor Silver. "The 'D' I gave you stands for 'dumb', and you've just earned it. The overtrick you let me make will get you the same zero you got for the previous two hands."

"What the @*&#@ are you talking about." I ask politely.

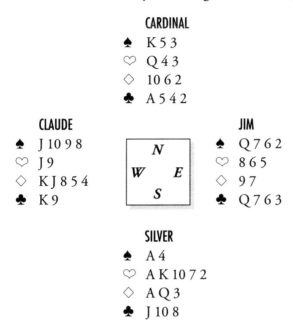

CARDINAL
- ♠ K 5 3
- ♡ Q 4 3
- ◇ 10 6 2
- ♣ A 5 4 2

CLAUDE
- ♠ J 10 9 8
- ♡ J 9
- ◇ K J 8 5 4
- ♣ K 9

JIM
- ♠ Q 7 6 2
- ♡ 8 6 5
- ◇ 9 7
- ♣ Q 7 6 3

SILVER
- ♠ A 4
- ♡ A K 10 7 2
- ◇ A Q 3
- ♣ J 10 8

"Look at the hands:"

"Ducking the ♣Q was intelligent, but you knew I wasn't going to guess wrong. I need a doubleton honour on my left to make two club tricks and the odds don't change whether my spot is the eight or the deuce. But when I threw you in, you thought I had forgotten to draw your last trump, didn't you? So you led a diamond through me to get a ruff. You couldn't see past the FREE BIRDSEED sign again.

"How was I getting two diamond tricks if your partner had any missing the missing honours behind me? Only if you endplayed him by leaving dummy with a trump. When he won the diamond jack he had to return one or give me a ruff and sluff. But if you had returned a heart, he could have safely exited with a spade whenever he won a diamond trick.

" Thanks for the top!"

THE COLLEGE BRIDGE PLAYER'S TOP FIVE BULIMIA LIST

1. Playing bridge with Professor Silver.
2. Playing bridge against Professor Silver.
3. Listening to Professor Silver lecture on bridge.
4. Giving Professor Silver a top board.
5. Listening to Professor Silver discourse on any topic.

"Tell me guys," says Wright Cardinal, obviously changing the subject, "is Professor Silver as good a teacher as he, I mean they, say he is?"

"You must understand, sir, that because of the recent cutbacks to college funding all the professors are overworked." Professor Silver leans back smiling fondly in my direction as I continue. "Such time as he can spare from playing bridge is devoted to the neglect of his duties. He is a disembodied cortex afloat in a Petrie dish of vanity. Do you know anyone else who is loathed by all who come in contact with him?"

"Actually, I could point out several playing in this room as we speak. But aren't you being just a little unfair because of your bad results on this round?"

Throwing caution to the winds, I continue. "Take this round as an example of his professional technique. Did he explain our mistakes so that we could learn something about the finer points of the game? No. He revelled in my embarrassment, to which he contributed by comparing my play to some double-dummy olympian level of skill to which only he dare aspire. No wonder young people are turning away from bridge. Do we ever get any encouragement? No. All we get are Pleistocene fossils amusing themselves at our expense."

"Get a life!" scowls Claude as we leave the table. As we move on Professor Silver leans forward and whispers something to Wright Cardinal. I can just make out what he is saying.

"There you can see, Cardinal, the future hope of the world, and of bridge. Remind me to change his 'D' to an 'F'.

AN OCCURRENCE AT THE SPINGOLD

The match was slipping away from us. Not an unusual occurrence in my long bridge career, but because of the circumstances, the pressure was unrelenting. I was playing with Wright Cardinal in the final of the Spingold; our partners were Eric Murray and Bruce Gowdy. We had enjoyed unprecedented success in the preceding rounds but our opposition in the final round was exceptionally formidable. Three of North America's top professionals, Stephen, Crane, and Barry, playing with an unusually capable client, were putting up a tough fight. The first half had been a standoff, but in this set we had suffered several swings against us. Now there was only one board left and I estimated that we were 20 IMPs down.

Wright was nervous. He examined his scorecard, glanced at our partners at the other table, and looked around for the closest exit. I, too, was apprehensive. From Bruce's demeanour, it was obvious that things had been going well at their table; I did not anticipate a tranquil comparison of scores. But, as Yogi Berra once observed under similar circumstances, "It ain't over till it's over".

I picked up the last hand.

$$\spadesuit K64 \quad \heartsuit 932 \quad \diamondsuit K107 \quad \clubsuit Q654$$

I was considerably relieved to hear Wright open the bidding with 2♣! We commenced an involved and scientific auction against which Stephen and Crane put up a barrage of interference, but to no avail. Having interposed a spade call or two, they began doubling each of our bids as their turn came. Ignoring them, we pressed on to our club slam, which to my surprise was again doubled. I was just about to redouble when, uncharacteristically, it occurred to me to ask for a review.

"Certainly," said Stephen, "I opened the bidding with one spade and your partner overcalled two clubs. Then....."

I didn't listen to the rest. I wondered whether I would be permitted a cigarette and blindfold before I had to face Bruce and Eric. Wright looked across the table at me, concerned.

"Are you all right, David?" he enquired, in a worried tone.

I felt dizzy and light-headed, but the game had to go on. I recovered my composure, passed the double of 6♣ and Crane led the ♡Q.

Suddenly Stephen sat up, a look of horror on his face. "Wait a minute," he said, "I've only got twelve cards!" Crane was discovered to have fourteen, and the director was called. The directors consulted briefly and ruled that the board would be thrown out.

"So the match is over," I remarked morosely to Cardinal.

"No, still three more to go," he replied, holding aloft the requisite number of boards. "Are you sure you're all right?"

Saved! And three chances remaining! A rush of adrenaline cleared my head and I replied "I'm terrific! I feel again a spark of that ancient flame. Let's stop talking and start playing bridge."

I picked up the next hand.

♠9 7 4 3 2 ♡ J 9 ◇ A K 9 ♣ Q 8 3

The bidding proceeded:

West	North	East	South
STEPHEN	CARDINAL	CRANE	SILVER
	1NT[1]	pass	2♣[2]
pass	2◇	pass	3♠
pass	3NT	pass	4♠[3]
all pass			

1. 12-14 points
2. Non-forcing Stayman
3. I'll fall on my own sword, thank you!

The opening lead was the ◇Q; Wright put the dummy down and I had to take ten tricks against expert defenders.

CARDINAL
- ♠ Q 10
- ♡ A K 6 4
- ◇ 7 5 3
- ♣ A J 4 2

SILVER
- ♠ 9 7 4 3 2
- ♡ J 9
- ◇ A K 9
- ♣ Q 8 3

I could see several routes to ten tricks but since every one depended on either an extraordinarily fortuitous lie of the cards and/or a misdefence, I abandoned each in turn. West wasn't going to hold a doubleton ♣K today!

If trumps did not lie favourably I was doomed (literally and figuratively speaking) so I presumed only two trump losers. At last, the winning line appeared to me like the angel at the Battle of Mons. I won the ◇K and led my ♡J. LHO covered with the queen and I let him hold the trick as East followed with the ♡7!

After a few moments LHO played a low spade to dummy's ten and East's king. Back came a low spade and dummy's queen won West's jack. "No wonder these boys have thousands of master points" I muttered to myself as I cashed the ♡A noting the fall of East's eight. The ♡K came next, East following with the ten as I discarded my losing diamond. Dummy's ♡6 was now high and I called for it to be played. RHO discarded a diamond and I threw away my ♣Q, ensuring two dummy entries. Warming to the task, I returned to my hand via the ◇A and finessed dummy's ♣J, and when it held I ruffed dummy's diamond as RHO threw a club. A club to the ace and a club back forced RHO to ruff in with his ♠A8 as I sat over him with my ♠97. Making four spades.

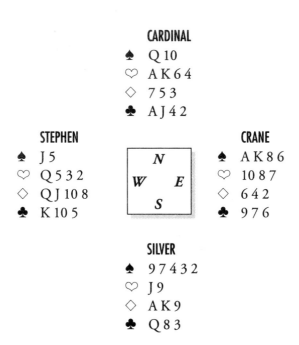

CARDINAL
♠ Q 10
♡ A K 6 4
◇ 7 5 3
♣ A J 4 2

STEPHEN
♠ J 5
♡ Q 5 3 2
◇ Q J 10 8
♣ K 10 5

CRANE
♠ A K 8 6
♡ 10 8 7
◇ 6 4 2
♣ 9 7 6

SILVER
♠ 9 7 4 3 2
♡ J 9
◇ A K 9
♣ Q 8 3

"I should have cashed the ♠A and returned the ♡10," said Crane.

"It wouldn't have changed anything," I said, consolingly. "I would simply cash the two top hearts. If you ruff the ♡6, I overruff and play spades, squeezing Stephen in diamonds and clubs. If you don't ruff, the play is essentially the same.   The hand can't be beaten as long as I throw the ♣Q so Stephen can't jump in with his king and block one of my dummy entries."

I could feel the momentum of the match swinging towards us, and eagerly, I picked up the penultimate hand:

♠ K J 7 ♡ A 7 3 ◇ 10 4 ♣ K Q J 9 8

The bidding proceeded:

West	North	East	South
STEPHEN	CARDINAL	CRANE	SILVER
1◇	1NT	pass	3♣[1]
pass	3◇	pass	6♣[2]
all pass			

1. Natural slam try
2. A better chance than 6NT, since I shall be on play

West led the ◇K and Wright laid down an adequate, if somewhat disappointing dummy.

♠ A 4 2
♡ K 10 4
◇ A 9 7
♣ A 10 4 3

♠ K J 7
♡ A 7 3
◇ 10 4
♣ K Q J 9 8

I paused, considered my strategy, and claimed twelve tricks.

"A straightforward progressive squeeze without the count," I announced. "Haven't seen one since Percy Sheardown played seven diamonds doubled in the 1958 Olympiad. Throw your cards in, boys, there's no defence."

Stephen looked puzzled. "Do you mind stating a line of play, please?" he asked.

"If you insist," I replied, "but I should have thought it was fairly obvious.

"Your modern-style aggressive light opening has marked you with all the remaining high cards — a meagre eleven points. Knowing that, I simply win the ◇A and run five rounds of clubs, throwing a spade from the dummy, and watching your discards for queens and jacks.

"Let's suppose you keep all your major suit cards and throw the $\diamond$J: I'll duck a diamond to your now-stiff queen, establishing my $\diamond$9 as trick eleven, and endplaying you in the majors for trick twelve. Either you'll lead a spade into me, or you'll lead a heart honour and set up a finessing position in the dummy.

"If I don't see you throw any honours, however, I know that your last seven cards are $\spadesuit$Q $\heartsuit$QJ $\diamond$QJ and two spot cards, so either spades or hearts are now unguarded. I lay down the $\heartsuit$A, and if the $\heartsuit$J falls, I can finesse the $\heartsuit$10 — just in case you are false-carding with three of them. Now I cash the $\heartsuit$K, and you'll have to unguard the $\spadesuit$Q or throw the $\diamond$J, allowing me to concede a diamond to establish trick twelve once again.

"If you follow small on the $\heartsuit$A, of course, I know the $\spadesuit$Q must be falling, so I cash three spades and once again you are forced to give up either the $\diamond$J or the heart suit."

"I'm sorry to have questioned you, Professor," said Stephen respectfully.

"Oh, that's all right," I replied magnanimously. "Of course, when I was your age, Sami Kehela would claim and everyone would throw their cards in. Then we'd stay up all night trying to work out how he would have played the hand. Tedious, but that's what made me the player I am today."

I moved confidently to the last hand:

$\spadesuit$ K J 8 7 $\heartsuit$ A 9 6 $\diamond$ K Q 5 $\clubsuit$ 10 8 7

The bidding proceed briskly:

West	North	East	South
STEPHEN	CARDINAL	CRANE	SILVER
			1NT[1]
pass	4NT	pass	6NT[2]
all pass			

1. 12-14 points
2. This *is* a maximum, since I could hold as little as 12 hcp; besides, I'm playing it.

The opening lead was the ♡3 and I was not displeased with the dummy.

CARDINAL
- ♠ A 5 4
- ♡ K J
- ◇ A J 10 4
- ♣ A K 9 2

SILVER
- ♠ K J 8 7
- ♡ A 9 6
- ◇ K Q 5
- ♣ 10 8 7

I played the ♡J which was covered by the queen and won by my ace. A low spade to the ace revealed nothing, but when I returned the suit and finessed the jack, LHO played the nine. I then ran the ♣10, losing to the jack on my right. Back came the ♡7; I won my ace as West followed with the ♡2, and I claimed the balance of the tricks.

"Meaning no disrespect, professor, I just don't see it," said Stephen, confused.

"Well, my boy, keep playing and studying and someday you will. But we're all tired, so I'll explain.

(see over for diagram)

"At this point, I shall cash four diamonds, throwing a club from my hand.. If spades are 3-3, I have the rest; if not, East who is known to have the ♠Q, must guard that suit, and can therefore hold on to only two clubs. West can temporarily guard clubs, but when I lead a spade to the king, he is squeezed in hearts and clubs: a simple non-simultaneous double squeeze. The exact position of the club suit is completely irrelevant."

CARDINAL

♠ 5
♡ —
♢ A J 10 4
♣ A K 9

```
      N
  W       E
      S
```

SILVER

♠ K 8
♡ 9
♢ K Q 5
♣ 8 7

The pros left dejectedly, and we were soon joined by Bruce and Eric. They had not had a good round, but it didn't matter: we had won handily, as a result of picking up 40 IMPs on those last three boards. Cardinal whooped and pumped my hand. Eric and Bruce looked sheepish and congratulated me on my performance.

"Just playing my usual game" I said as I turned to accept the congratulations of the kibitzers. The news spread like wildfire. Strangers were shaking my hand and clasping my elbow. A nubile sixty-year-old whispered something in my ear and pressed her room key in my palm. The din was deafening, the room suddenly extremely hot and crowded, and I felt faint and dizzy, grasping at Wright's arm to keep from falling.

"Are you all right, David?" he enquired, in a worried tone.

"Yes, thank you, I just felt faint for a moment."

"In that case, would you mind putting the dummy down? We'd like to finish the last hand so we can all go home."

I looked up at Wright, waiting impatiently. Crane looked at me quizzically, the ♡Q on the table in front of him. Standing out in the corridor I could see a smiling Bruce and Eric waiting restively to compare scores.

"What's the contract?"

"Six clubs doubled. Now, can we see your hand?"

Wright took his five club tricks and that was that, seven down doubled, vulnerable. Our opponents left quickly and silently and we were joined by our partners.

"Don't look so worried, guys, we'll be fine as long as you didn't go for any numbers," said Bruce jovially as he sat down.

There is no armour against fate. I fumbled with my convention card and quietly moved my chair back a few inches. Wright began calling out our scores, and I slowly rose to my feet and ran like hell.

THE FOUR FEATHERS

The 1960 Bridge Olympiad!" said Bruce Gowdy to an enthralled audience of rookies. "Bridge was bridge in those days. Legends at every table: Reese and Schapiro, Goren and Sobel, Jacoby, Schenken. Tough, expert bridge players all, not like the pseudo-scientific wimps you see nowadays. Professor Silver! Do you remember the hand that finished off the Americans in the quarter-finals?"

"Only too well, Bruce. For thirty-six years you've been telling that story to everyone who has ventured within earshot, and you have a loud voice," said Silver, with a wink in my direction.

"Do let him tell it again, Professor," said Mia Culpa. "It's a great hand and I never get tired of hearing it."

"It was a dark and stormy match. The Americans had been bouncing the Professor and me around as if we were basketballs. But on the last hand, we bid a grand slam which required me to invent what become known as a 'Gowdy Ending'"

"What's a Gowdy Ending?" asked one of the rookies.

"That's where you make a grand slam by squeezing the opponents and setting up the deuce of clubs as your thirteenth trick," replied another rookie smugly. "Everybody knows that."

"Quite right! Quite right! Bright lad, isn't he?" said Bruce. "I arrived in 7♡, the bidding isn't important, and needless to say, when the dummy hit the table I was a trick short of thirteen.

DUMMY		BRUCE
♠ A 4 2		♠ K 5 3
♡ Q 10 9 8	N	♡ A K J 7 6 4 3
◇ 7 6 5 4	W E	◇ A
♣ A K 2	S	♣ 9 8

"The ◇K was led," Bruce continued, "and I studied the dummy for a long time, almost twenty seconds, before finding the winning line. After winning the ◇A I crossed to dummy's ♡Q; both opponents followed, and I cashed the ♡10 before ruffing a diamond high as LHO played the queen. Now I went to the dummy with the ♠A and ruffed another diamond as RHO discarded a small spade. Then I cashed the ♠K, and both opponents followed. It was at that moment that I announced..."

"The deuce of clubs will be my thirteenth trick!" chanted Professor Silver, Eric Murray, and I in unison.

"Quite right! Quite right, guys. I ran my trumps, and this was the end position:

DUMMY		BRUCE
♠ —		♠ 5
♡ —	N	♡ 3
◇ 7	W E	◇ —
♣ A K 2	S	♣ 9 8

"I led my last heart and LHO, forced to keep a diamond, discarded a club. I discarded dummy's now useless diamond and RHO, who had to guard spades, also threw a club. I now cashed dummy's ♣AK and the club deuce, as I had predicted, had become my thirteenth trick! Needless to say, the opponents at the other table bid and made only six hearts. We won the match by 4 IMPs."

As always, the story drew gasps of admiration from someone who had not heard it, and soon afterwards, the party broke up.

"Gentlemen, a word!" I said to my team-mates as everyone prepared to leave Mia's suite. "I have an announcement to make. I have to tell you that I am unable to play the Knockout final tomorrow."

"Why ever not?" asked Bruce.

"I, er, I must go to a job interview."

"A job interview?" asked Professor Silver, justifiably astounded. "But you committed yourself to playing on our team!"

" Now, I know playing against those juniors will be scary," said Bruce, "but just go home and get some sleep. You'll be okay in the morning."

"No, I've made up my mind, Mia will take my place; she's on the team roster anyway as npc. I'm going to get that job."

My three erstwhile team-mates stared at me in varying attitudes of horror, dismay, and disbelief, and then attempted for some time to dissuade me. This was not, however, a decision I had reached lightly, and I remained steadfast. Eventually they abandoned their efforts, and removed themselves to the bar to discuss the unexpected turn of events, leaving Mia and me alone in her suite.

"Wright Cardinal, just what do you think you're doing? They were counting on you." cried Mia.

"Mia, we've often spoken of the pointlessness of spending our lives playing bridge, living from hand to mouth, never seeing the light of day. I want to have a job, make some friends. I want to get a life."

At that moment, a knock came at the door. When I answered it, one of the rookies without a word handed me an envelope and left. Inside were three white feathers, each with a business card attached. I read the names aloud. "Eric Murray, Bruce Gowdy, David Silver".

I stared at them and turned to Mia. "White feathers! They think I'm scared to play the match against the juniors tomorrow!"

"Of course they do. Sure, Wright, we've often spoken of what we might do if we were free. But you and I are not free. We're bridge players, and we have commitments to partners and team-mates who are affected if we don't live up to our obligations. Did you think I would be proud of you when you chickened out of a tough match? Sending you those feathers was cruel, but think how disappointed in you those guys must be."

"If you feel like that," I replied, "then there should be a fourth feather — yours."

I strode over to the bird cage, reached in, and tore a feather from the budgie's tail. Ignoring the squawks emanating from both Mia and the budgie, I thrust the feather into Mia's hand.

"Give it to me, Mia. If you, too, think me a coward, give it to me."

She held it out without a word, and I thrust her feather with the other three into my pocket. We parted in silence.

During the sleepless night that followed, I finally admitted to myself that my true motives were in fact base and that I was indeed the despicable coward my team-mates thought me. Perhaps it was not too late to make amends: I hastened to the tournament and showed up to play.

I was accepted on the condition that Bruce, Eric, and the professor would take turns playing with me. The unspoken implication was that none of them wanted to spend the afternoon partnering a wretch who had so nearly let the side down.

I played the first quarter with Eric Murray in an uncomfortable silence. The only sound was the slapping of cards on the table, since the use of bidding boxes, thankfully, made oral communication superfluous.

Towards the end of the set I picked up:

♠ A K J 10 9 8 ♡ K ◇ K 9 7 5 ♣ 5 2

Both sides were vulnerable and I opened the bidding in first chair with 1♠. LHO overcalled with 2♡, Eric jumped to 3♠, and RHO passed. Eric's 3♠ bid showed a limit raise and I contemplated passing it with my effective 11-count, but the lure of a vulnerable game was too tempting to resist. I bid four and everyone passed.

My left hand opponent led a trump, as she always does unless void in the trump suit. The dummy appeared and I counted my tricks. It didn't take long.

MURRAY			CARDINAL
♠ 4 3 2			♠ A K J 10 9 8
♡ J 5 3	N		♡ K
◇ 6 2	W E		◇ K 9 7 5
♣ A K Q 9 4	S		♣ 5 2

I had bought a fine dummy, but I could see that problems would arise if spades did not divide 2-2. South had found the excellent (for them) lead of a trump without which I could just have given up two diamonds, ruffed one in the dummy, and discarded the fourth on the queen of clubs. Dummy's small spade spots precluded any thoughts of a late entry to the club suit if that, too, didn't split and the vulnerable overcall by West boded ill for any chance of the ◇A being on my right.

With a sense of impending doom I drew trumps, watching North discard hearts on the second and third rounds, and played the ♣AKQ. On the ♣Q both South and I discarded, she a heart and I a diamond. Fighting back tears of despair I ruffed dummy's small club; I had established the ♣9 as a trick, but how could I get there with no dummy entry?

Suddenly I realized that LHO could be used as a stepping stone to the dummy. I laid down the ♡K, won by South's ace. She now played the ♡Q, upon which I discarded a small diamond! South was now endplayed: a heart to dummy's jack would give me the dummy, and an overtrick, while a diamond lead would establish my king for the game-going trick.

"Gutsy bid, Wright, nicely played," said Eric, smiling suddenly. He accepted his feather back when I offered it to him, and the rest of the hands were played out in a friendly and cordial atmosphere.

However, neither cordial nor friendly were words I could use to describe Bruce Gowdy's demeanour when I played with him in the second quarter. He loomed over me like the sword of Damocles, ready to impale me for any trangression, real or imagined. Fate, however, confronted me on the third hand. Our vulnerable opponents had arrived in 3NT on the auction: 1♣ by LHO, 1◇ by RHO, 1NT by the opener, 2NT by responder, 3NT, passed around to me. I looked again at my hand.

♠ K 5 ♡ 10 7 6 5 ◇ K Q 10 8 ♣ J 7 4

Almost any lead from Bruce seemed likely to give declarer a trick and/or a tempo. Did I dare double for a diamond lead? They might redouble and make the contract with overtricks. I shut my eyes and doubled anyway. Everyone passed and Bruce led the ♢4. A distressingly strong dummy was put on the table.

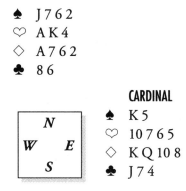

♠ J 7 6 2
♡ A K 4
♢ A 7 6 2
♣ 8 6

CARDINAL
♠ K 5
♡ 10 7 6 5
♢ K Q 10 8
♣ J 7 4

Declarer played low from the dummy and I won the queen. Attacking what I hoped was a chink in the opponents' armour, I put the ♣J down — and everyone followed low. I continued clubs. Declarer contemplated my ♣7 for a while and finally played the king. Bruce grabbed his ace and cashed the queen and two more small clubs. He exited with the ♢3, won by dummy's ace. Declarer now played a spade towards her hand, successfully finessing the queen. When the ♠A felled my doubleton king, declarer claimed the balance, thankful to escape for only two down, vulnerable.

Later, when we were comparing scores with our partners, we learned that Professor Silver had made three notrumps as declarer on this hand *(see hand diagram on next page)*.

In the absence of a lead-directing double, West had led a club, which the professor had won in hand with the king. Crossing to dummy's ♡A, he had finessed against East's ♠K, and made nine tricks when it fell under his ace; three spades, four hearts, the ♢A and the ♣K. The 15-IMP pickup gave us the lead in the match!

"Nice double, Wright," said Eric, "Not an easy bid to make when you're playing with a volatile partner."

"I would have applauded the bid, even if we had lost 15 IMPs instead of gaining them." Bruce protested. "It was a well-thought-out tactical double; nicely done, Wright!"

MURRAY
♠ J 7 6 2
♡ A K 4
◇ A 7 6 2
♣ 8 6

♠ 10 9 4 3
♡ 9 3
◇ 4 3
♣ A Q 10 9 5

♠ K 5
♡ 10 7 6 5
◇ K Q 10 8
♣ J 7 4

SILVER
♠ A Q 8
♡ Q J 8 2
◇ J 9 5
♣ K 3 2

He took my hand and shook it vigorously, then grinned at the sight of his feather which I had left in his palm. He put the feather in his wallet and we all returned to the fray. Now holding a slight lead, we were scheduled to revert to our established partnerships, and I sat down opposite the stern visage of Professor Silver.

I had won back the good opinion of my other two team-mates, but Professor Silver was unrelenting. He spoke not a word to me for eight hands, although I tried several times to start a conversation. His play was prenaturally sharp and I had to concentrate fully in order to follow the delicate nuances of his bids and signals. I dared not relax even for a second.

Then I was dealer on what was certain to be a hand fraught with danger:

♠ A K 2 ♡ K Q 7 4 2 ◇ A 5 4 ♣ K 2

The immediate problem was that I had to bid the heart suit first. Professor Silver considers the heart suit to be his personal property by *droit de seigneur*. Consequently, I would have to arrive at not just a reasonable contract, but the double-dummy correct level at which to play. Any error in bidding judgment would be tantamount to suicide. On the bright side, Professor Silver might bid spades or notrumps, both of which I could support vigorously.

It was not to be. I opened with 1♡ and the professor and I quickly propelled ourselves into 6♡. West led the ◇Q and I was pleased with the dummy. It looked as though twelve tricks would be easy.

SILVER
♠ 9 6 3
♡ A 6 3
◇ K 6 3 2
♣ A Q 6

CARDINAL
♠ A K 2
♡ K Q 7 4 2
◇ A 5 4
♣ K 2

I should have known better. I counted my tricks three times. There was one inescapable loser, but the rest of the tricks were there if the heart suit behaved. My heart spots were so weak as to preclude any hope of picking up a four-card holding in the West hand, so I won the diamond in hand and cashed the ♡Q. Everyone followed suit, but when I continued with the ♡K, West showed out! Faced now with the dreaded 4-1 trump split, I desperately sought a lie of cards that would permit me to make a slam while holding two certain losers! Professor Silver, noting my sudden pallor, looked at me suspiciously and I knew that he would certainly find a winning line of play at the post mortem. I had better discover one at the table or suffer his scathing criticism later.

I realized that indeed there was still a chance to make the contract, if only RHO would follow to three clubs, two spades, and two diamonds. I played three rounds of clubs, carefully pitching a diamond on the ♣Q. Now I cashed my two spade tricks before East had a chance to pitch one from a doubleton. The $\diamond$K was played, and when this lived, I was in excellent shape. We had arrived at this position:

SILVER
- ♠ 3
- ♡ A
- ♢ 6 3
- ♣ —

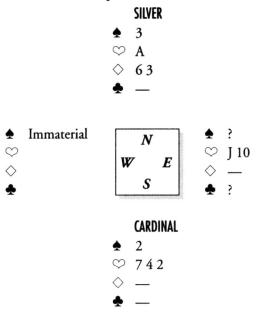

♠ Immaterial
♡
♢
♣

♠ ?
♡ J 10
♢ —
♣ ?

CARDINAL
- ♠ 2
- ♡ 7 4 2
- ♢ —
- ♣ —

I called for a small diamond from the dummy. East realized that if he ruffed I would throw my small spade, so he discarded as I ruffed in hand. Now I was able to cross once again to the ♡A, which with fortuitous foresight I had left in the dummy. Everyone was down to two cards. I held the deuces of spades and hearts. But the lead was in dummy and I was able to lead the last diamond through East. Faced again with Hobson's choice, he conceded the slam. If he ruffed in, I would discard my spade and take the last trick with my ♡2 If he discarded, I could ruff the diamond for my twelfth trick and he would ruff his partner's spade winner on the last round.

"*En passant, mon cher Cardinal,*" said Professor Silver. "A lesser player would have given up after the bad trump break, but you bravely persevered and found the winning line. Well done! By the way, I believe you have on your person something that belongs to me?"

He extended his hand into which I deposited his white feather. To the astonishment of everyone but me, he calmly proceeded to eat it, apparently savouring every morsel. "Well, at least it wasn't a crow's feather," he remarked. We finished the rest of the session with our old relationship restored, and we won the match.

A crowd gathered again in Mia's suite as we relaxed afterwards with Bruce and Eric. Bruce sat down with a group of rookies and addressed his attentive listeners.

"The 1960 Bridge Olympiad!" he began. "Bridge was bridge in those days. Legends at every table...."

I raised my glass to greet a smiling Mia.

"Wright, you're not finished yet. What incredible feat of skill and daring will get me to take back my feather?"

"Must I?"

"Of course you must. This story has to end with the hero regaining his girl's respect and esteem."

"Follow me," I said, leading her over to where Bruce was regaling his audience with the famous story. He got to his famous line "The deuce of clubs will be my thirteenth trick!", and I interrupted.

"Bruce — you never said it."

"What? What on earth are you talking about?" Bruce expostulated.

"You never said it. You will recall that Sami Kehela, who was sitting out for that set, was watching your match. Sami, although arguably the best bridge player of the era, always conceded that he could never match your prowess handling the dummy and kibitzed you every time the opportunity presented itself."

"Quite right! Quite right!"

"On this occasion, he recalls, tension was high and you played the hand in complete silence, focusing on each card as it was played. And you played it brilliantly, winning the match for your team and glory for yourself. But you never said 'The deuce of clubs will be my thirteenth trick'. You never said anything at all. Come on now, Bruce, confess — or are you going to call Sami a liar?"

"But, but..." spluttered Bruce. "Confound you, Cardinal, I'll never be able to tell that story again!"

"Mia — your feather."

THE PRISONER OF ZELDA

Fortunately, I had bought the newspapers, for I found in them news which immediately affected my plans. For some reason which was not clearly explained, the date of the Ruritanian Invitational Team Tournament had suddenly been advanced and the first match was to take place on the next day but one. The whole populace had been in a stir about it since His Majesty's Ambassador to Canada had confirmed that Professor Silver had condescended to form a team and to represent his country.

It was evident that Streslau, the capital, would be thronged. The reporter warned that all rooms were let and the hotels overflowing, so there would be little chance of my obtaining lodging. Despite being in my eighty-second year, I decided to make bivouac in Zelda, a small town fifty miles short of Streslau, and to go by train to and from the site of the tournament. No Ruritanian would stay in Zelda after dusk, so accommodations should be plentiful and cheap. Fortune favoured me; I quickly secured suitable rooms in Zelda, and set off towards Streslau for an evening's kibitzing.

Clutching my dog-eared copy of *Das Bridge: die folgrechte Silverordnung* I disembarked on to the station platform at Streslau to be immediately accosted by two foreigners. The large one, a young fellow in his mid-sixties, grasped my elbow and began addressing me as "Professor Silver" while chattering excitedly to his companion in what I assumed was English. The smaller one peered myopically at me and responded calmly to the giant's increasingly agitated discourse. They obviously had no German and I despaired of communication until I noticed they were wearing badges displaying a red maple leaf on a white background, the insignia of Canada. I remembered that Canada was officially bilingual and that all Canadians were required by law to speak fluent French.

"*Messieurs, je crois que vous êtes en erreur,*" I said coldly. "While I have the honour to be related to the great man, I regret I am not he. I am his nephew, Fritz von Zelber, retired Colonel of His Majesty's Household Guards. *Oui,* Professor Silver is by birth a Ruritanian — his real name is Sigmund von Zelber. His family emigrated to Canada in 1920 shortly after the Great War, anglicized their name and settled there. That was the last we heard of him until the German translation of his book, *Bridge the Silver Way,* appeared a few years ago and made him the national hero of Ruritania.

"A national hero?"

"Bridge was introduced into the country by the same American soldiers who restored our monarchy in 1945 and has been our national pastime ever since. Professor Silver's book, and its exhilarating theory of *Blitzkrieg Gespraachen*, Pre-emptive First Strike Bidding, established *die folgrechte Silverordnung* as the national bidding system. Everyone plays it, except for a tiny minority of traditionalists who still play Goren.

"His Majesty, King Rudolf, decided to observe the fiftieth anniversary of our national sport by holding a commemorative tournament with a generous cash prize to the winners. Ruritania is one of Canada's principal creditors, so His Majesty was able to persuade the Canadian Bridge Federation to send Professor Silver's team to participate. But *mon dieu!* Surely I recognize you, sir — do I have the honour of addressing Wright Cardinal?"

"*Oui, mon colonel,* and may I introduce my countryman, Bruce Gowdy," replied the shorter stranger. "We are in urgent of need your help. Professor Silver has been kidnapped by a terrorist group of bridge fundamentalists, *die Gorenanhängerin.* They are demanding a ransom of 100,000 Canadian dollars for his release. We have appealed to the Canadian bridge community for contributions but the tournament starts this afternoon and we shall have to forfeit if we don't field a team. Your resemblance to Professor Silver is striking, so perhaps we can prevail upon you to impersonate him until we can obtain his release."

"It won't work," scowled the giant. "The colonel can't speak English and is obviously much younger than David."

"Relax, Bruce, you're forgetting that all Silver's books carry a picture of him taken in the 1950's so none of the locals would recognize the genuine professor. We're using bidding boxes so it won't matter what languages he can or cannot speak. My only worry is that the Colonel is too intelligent to pass as Silver, but we have to chance it."

I could not, of course, resist such a plea from a fellow bridge player in distress, not to mention the chance for me, a *lumpenspieler*, to take the legendary Professor Silver's place, playing with his favourite partner in an international match, with Bruce Gowdy and Eric Murray at the other table. It was soon settled; for a day, at least, I would become Professor Silver.

In the event, the secret of my imposture defied detection. I had bad moments, of course: it needed all of Herr Gowdy's tact and graciousness to smooth over some apparent lapses of memory and un-mindfulness of old acquaintances of which I was inevitably guilty. But I survived, and I attribute my escape most of all to the very audacity of the enterprise.

We compared scores at the half and we were winning by several IMPs. There had been a communication from the terrorists informing us that they were playing bridge with Professor Silver to occupy the time until the midnight deadline and, inexplicably, that they had reduced their ransom demand to fifty Canadian dollars. At this, Bruce and Wright exchanged knowing glances and we returned for the second half of the match.

Up until now, the play had been largely uneventful. My bidding had been confined to raising Cardinal's trump suit, and avoiding bidding notrumps. My few gaffes had been more than compensated for by my partner's prowess in dummy handling, but I felt unfulfilled. I longed to implement the principles outlined in *Bridge the Silver Way*, especially *Die Überlegenheit der herzen Farbekennen*, the supremacy of the heart suit. I did not enlist in order to cower under cover, I came to fight, and later in the match my opportunity arose. I picked up the following hand and as Goethe put it, *Amboss oder Hammer sein*. Tired of being an anvil, I became a hammer; I bid the hand as if I were Professor Silver:

♠ A K Q 7 5 3   ♡ A J 6   ♢ 2   ♣ 7 4 2

West	North	East	South
	CARDINAL		**VON ZELBER**
		pass	1♡ [1]
pass	2♡ [2]	pass	4NT [3]
pass	5♠ [4]	pass	6♡ [5]
all pass			

1. Straight out of 'BTSW'
2. Inverted major raise; 'BTSW' page 1024
3. Keycard Blackwood
4. 2 keycards and the ♡Q
5. Let them find the club lead.....

A triumph for *die folgrechte Silverordnung*! The two hands were:

CARDINAL
- ♠ 6 4 2
- ♡ K Q 4 2
- ◇ 8 6 3
- ♣ A J 5

VON ZELBER
- ♠ A K Q 7 5 3
- ♡ A J 6
- ◇ 2
- ♣ 7 4 2

The play was simple when the defence started with the ace and king of diamonds: I ruffed the second diamond and laid down the ace and jack of hearts. Crossing to the ♣A, I discarded my two losing clubs on the king and queen of hearts and claimed the balance — plus 1430! Later, I found out that our inexpert opponents had bid to four spades, making five. Flushed with success, I picked up the next hand:

♠ — ♡ K 10 3 ◇ A 7 5 4 3 ♣ A Q 6 4 2

Ach du Lieber! What would Professor Silver bid? The answer was soon forthcoming:

West	North	East	South
	CARDINAL		VON ZELBER
			1♡[1]
1♠	2♡[2]	3♠	4♡[3]
all pass			

1. 'BTSW' page 1 et passim
2. Inverted major raise
3. Herr Cardinal will play the wheels off it!

To my horror, LHO led the ♠A and I remembered that I had bid hearts first. The dummy was disappointing but I did see a winning line if the distribution were favourable.

CARDINAL

♠ Q 6 5 3
♡ A Q J
◇ J 8 6 2
♣ K 7

VON ZELBER

♠ —
♡ K 10 3
◇ A 7 5 4 3
♣ A Q 6 4 2

I ruffed the opening spade lead and crossed to the ♣K. I ruffed another spade with my ♡10. The ♣A and ♣Q both lived and I cashed my

$\diamond$A. I now ruffed a fourth club with dummy's $\heartsuit$A and led a third spade, ruffed with my $\heartsuit$K. I had scored one diamond, three clubs, three hearts in my hand and one in the dummy — eight tricks! Since dummy's $\heartsuit$QJ ensured tricks nine and ten, I claimed my contract.

Happily, the opponents' comments were interrupted by the arrival of a courier, and we took a short break to discuss the latest proposal from the *Gorenanhängerin*. Their letter, which I translated from German, was short and to the point. They were willing to drop their ransom demand and return Professor Silver immediately, if we would come and take him back. He was being held at Castle Zelda but he was refusing to leave until his captors fully understood his bidding system. Wright, over my protestations, instructed me to write a reply stating that we would accept Professor Silver only on payment of $500 in US funds, cash on the barrelhead!

"Such dedication," I said to myself. "Imagine the courage of the man to proselytize his kidnappers while in mortal danger!" But my reveries were interrupted when LHO opened the bidding with 1$\heartsuit$. Astounded by such audacity, I glanced at my cards. I held:

$\spadesuit$ A 6 2 $\heartsuit$ 5 3 2 $\diamond$ Q J 10 4 $\clubsuit$ A J 6

The bidding proceeded and at my turn, I had a problem:

West	North CARDINAL	East	South VON ZELBER
1$\heartsuit$ [1]	2$\clubsuit$	2$\heartsuit$	3$\heartsuit$ [2]
dbl	3NT	dbl	all pass

1. Impudent *auslander*!
2. Systemic — 'BTSW' page 34

I had some difficulty recalling the system's handling of heart bids by the opponents, but it came back to me in time for my first turn to bid. According to Professor Silver's 'Law of Subtotal Tricks', the level to which a partnership should compete was determined by the number of hearts held by the opponents. Therefore, I bid 3♡ to tell Herr Cardinal how many hearts I held. His 3NT bid was obviously intended as a save against their heart contract so I passed. LHO led a heart and Wright claimed nine tricks. The full deal was:

CARDINAL
- ♠ K 4 3
- ♡ A
- ♢ 7 5 2
- ♣ K Q 10 9 7 4

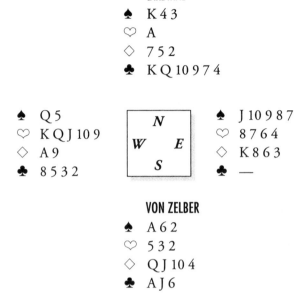

- ♠ Q 5
- ♡ K Q J 10 9
- ♢ A 9
- ♣ 8 5 3 2

- ♠ J 10 9 8 7
- ♡ 8 7 6 4
- ♢ K 8 6 3
- ♣ —

VON ZELBER
- ♠ A 6 2
- ♡ 5 3 2
- ♢ Q J 10 4
- ♣ A J 6

I pointed out to the opponents that they were cold for four hearts and urged them to buy copies of *Bridge the Silver Way*, as soon as possible. Despite the setbacks inflicted on them by these hands, our opponents showed their mettle by completely collapsing and the rest of the match was a virtual harvest of IMPs.

The score was tallied and reported in great haste as another courier had arrived with an envelope full of American dollars and directions to Castle Zelda. I urged Wright and Bruce to drive quickly to ensure Professor Silver's retrieval before sundown. They left hurriedly, but not before Herr Cardinal had paid me the supreme compliment of comparing my bidding to that of my distinguished relative.

Since all these events whose history I have set down happened, I have lived a very quiet life at a small house I have taken in the country. Sometimes I have a fancy — the superstitious would call it a presentiment — that my bridge career is not yet altogether complete; that somehow and someday, I shall play again in high-level matches. I shall again spin bids out of the Silver Method, brace my brain for a competitive auction, strike first with pre-emptive calls. Whether this fancy will be fulfilled I cannot tell, but I fervidly wish it may be, for I would love to see myself once again at the tournament at Streslau, watching the epic battle between Princess Flavia's team and Professor Silver's brave warriors, or hearing from one of the survivors about the climactic game within the frowning keep of Castle Zelda itself.

But in those tumultuous events I took no further part, and it is fitting that at this point I lay down my pen, and refer my patient readers to Wright Cardinal's own account of the following days.

A Scandal in Ruritania

To Professor Silver, she was always *the* woman; I have seldom heard him mention her under any other name. In his eyes she eclipses and predominates the whole of her sex. It was not that he felt an emotion akin to love for Mercilla Fortuna — all emotions, and that one particularly, were abhorrent to his cold, precise, but admirably balanced mind. He never spoke of the softer passions, save with a gibe and a sneer. They were admirable things for kibitzers and amateurs, but for the serious bridge player to admit such intrusions into his own finely adjusted temperament was to introduce a distracting factor which might disturb his concentration. And yet there was but one woman to him, and that woman was the late Mercilla Fortuna of dubious and questionable memory.

One night — it was the evening before our playing the final match of the Ruritanian Invitational Team Championships — I looked up from my favourite television show, *Baywatch*, to see Professor Silver's tall, spare, figure pass twice in a dark silhouette before the screen. He was pacing the room, swiftly, eagerly, his head sunk upon his chest and his hands clasped behind him. To me, who knew his every mood and habit, his attitude and manner told their own story: he was working out a bridge problem.

"I'm sorry to disturb you, Cardinal," he remarked, "I know how much you enjoy the intellectual repartee between the characters on that program."

"No matter, Professor," I replied, somewhat taken aback by his uncharacteristic sarcasm. "Since the dialogue is dubbed into German, I wasn't able to follow the story anyway."

"Quite so," he answered throwing himself down into an armchair. "Permit me to switch this machine off; there is a serious matter I must raise with you. You may not have realized, Cardinal, the importance of our winning this match tomorrow, but without the cash prize that accompanies the championship, we can't get home. The Canadian Bridge Federation provided the two of us with one-way tickets only, an oversight I'm sure, but they have not responded to my telegrams nor have they answered my phone calls. And I fear that neither Bruce nor Eric would lend us money even if they were speaking to us."

"But I don't think we have any cause for concern, Professor; Bruce and Eric are playing extremely well. After all, they've carried us through to the finals. And while you and I have had our difficulties, I'm sure we'll regain our form tomorrow. Besides, this isn't exactly the final round of the Spingold. We're playing this local team, Princess Flavia and her cousin, er....?"

"Mercilla."

"That's right. And the other pair, Count Alucard and that weird Renfrew person, they're not experts. We should blitz them easily! The only thing that concerns me is that the match begins at sundown and continues until daybreak! But you're an old rubber bridge player so the schedule shouldn't bother you."

"There's many a slip twixt the cup and the lip, Cardinal. You have obviously not considered the fact that they have beaten some very good teams on their path to potential humiliation at our hands. But you are correct in your assessment of their abilities. The situation is ...."

"Peculiar?"

"Peculiar — that is the very word. So peculiar that I have asked a member of the Egyptian team, who were beaten soundly by Princess Flavia's team this evening, to visit us tonight. Perhaps, with his help, we can gain some insight into our opponents' success. By the way, if you should recognize him, please respect his privacy. Answer the door, would you, that should be him now."

I opened the door and a man entered who could hardly have gone unrecognized in even the remotest part of the civilized world. Millions of fans had thrilled to his performances on the screen for more than thirty years. I, of course, knew that he was a world-class bridge player, but since he played only in Europe, I had never met him.

"Professor Silver, it's........"

"Mr. Ross, Cardinal, Mr. Ross ...... bringing us hands from his semi-final match, I believe"

Indeed he was, and after accepting Professor Silver's assurances as to my discretion the man who preferred to be known as 'Ross' drew a sheaf of papers from his pocket and spread them on the table. As he gazed fixedly at the hand records, for such they were, our visitor acquired a haunted look, and he said nothing until Professor Silver looked up impatiently.

"You can understand, gentlemen," began Ross, "that I am not accustomed to blaming losses on anything other than player error. Yet the circumstances of this last match are so bizarre that I cannot explain them! Our opponents seemed to have been gifted with second sight, bidding thin games when every finesse was on, and being always content with part scores when the cards were badly placed. Of course, there are sessions when opponents get what basketball players call "hot hands", but I have never before seen a pair that exhibited perfect judgment on every hand they bid or played."

"Surely you exaggerate, my dear Ross," said Professor Silver, languidly leaning back and closing his eyes. "The race is not always to the swift. Every bridge player in the world can provide anecdotal evidence for Silver's Second Law of Bridge, 'It's better to be lucky than smart' — right, Cardinal?"

"It sounds as though you've just met a team that played over their heads. Professor Silver and I recently lost a Regional under similar circumstances. They just overbid their hands and made everything. It happens sometimes when a weaker team despairs of outplaying its opponents and bids wildly."

"No, you don't understand. They don't just count on being lucky, they've actually incorporated luck into their bidding system."

At this, Professor Silver reopened his eyes and leaned forward.

"Please explain!" he demanded.

"The ladies, Princess Flavia and Countess Fortuna, play their own bidding system which they call the LOL System. Upon inquiring, I was informed that the acronym stands for 'Lots Of Luck'. That's basically all they have on their card, with the exception of those few conventions that any duplicate player might be familiar with. They even alert bids that are made on the presumption that the contract will be serendipitously makeable!

"At first we smiled politely at their naiveté, but as we played hand after hand, it became obvious that their system was 100% accurate! We were blitzed, of course, but I could find no grounds for protest. What rational complaints could I present to an appeals committee? Permit me to cite an example. Early in the match Mercilla held:

♠ 10 7 2   ♡ A 6   ◇ A K 5 2   ♣ A J 5 2

The bidding proceeded:

West	North	East	South
KHEDIVE	FLAVIA	ROSS	MERCILLA
			1NT
2♠	3NT[1]	pass	pass[2]
pass			

1. 'Fast' Lebensohl, denying a spade stopper
2. Alerted as an LOL pass

"Needless to say, the hand was unbeatable!"

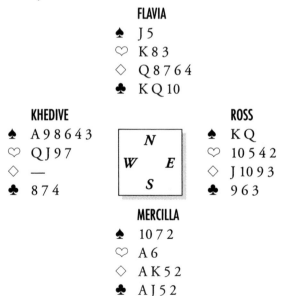

FLAVIA
♠ J 5
♡ K 8 3
◇ Q 8 7 6 4
♣ K Q 10

KHEDIVE
♠ A 9 8 6 4 3
♡ Q J 9 7
◇ —
♣ 8 7 4

ROSS
♠ K Q
♡ 10 5 4 2
◇ J 10 9 3
♣ 9 6 3

MERCILLA
♠ 10 7 2
♡ A 6
◇ A K 5 2
♣ A J 5 2

"You see, gentlemen, not only is the spade suit hopelessly blocked, but there are three diamonds, two hearts and four clubs — nine tricks — to be cashed as soon as I shift at trick three! Our partners reached the eminently sensible contract of 5♢, which failed by a trick because of the 4-0 trump split. But there's more: on the very next deal, Mercilla held.....

♠ A 6 3 2   ♡ K 5 4   ♢ K J 9 3   ♣ A 6

"Flavia opened with 1♢ and the bidding proceeded:

West	North	East	South
KHEDIVE	FLAVIA	ROSS	MERCILLA
	1♢	pass	1♠
pass	2♣	pass	2♡[1]
pass	2NT	pass	pass[2]
pass			

1. Fourth suit, forcing to game
2. Alerted as an LOL pass

"A prescient pass! There are only eight tricks available."

FLAVIA
♠   8 5
♡   A 7
♢   A 6 5 4 2
♣   K Q 7 5

KHEDIVE		ROSS
♠ Q 10 9 7 4	N	♠ K J
♡ Q J 8	W E	♡ 10 9 6 3 2
♢ Q 10 8 7	S	♢ —
♣ 3		♣ J 10 9 8 4 2

MERCILLA
♠   A 6 3 2
♡   K 5 4
♢   K J 9 3
♣   A 6

"Our partners, with 27 high card points, all suits stopped and a known 5-4 diamond fit, unaccountably bid 3NT, one down! Don't you agree,

Professor, that there is something going on here?"

"I've seen nothing so far that can't be attributed to blind chance. Permit me, but I have often written that top-flight pairs are distinguished from the herd by the number of slams they bid and make. Surely you are not suggesting that the ladies' crystal ball also directs them to unbeatable slams?"

"Yes!" replied Ross, wringing his hands. "Their system appears to work just as inexorably at the six and seven levels. Take Board 17; you are South, playing in 6♠ after opening the bidding 2♣. The opponents were silent and the opening lead is the ♡Q; try and make it."

"Elementary, my dear Ross. You see the obvious trap, of course, Cardinal? An ordinary player would win the opening lead and play

FLAVIA

♠ K 3
♡ 6 5
◇ 10 9 5 3
♣ Q 8 5 3 2

MERCILLA

♠ A Q J 10 9 6 2
♡ A K 7 2
◇ A K
♣ —

the ♡K preparatory to ruffing a heart in the dummy. Matchpoint players might even anticipate ruffing both heart losers for an overtrick. But what happens if the ♡K gets ruffed and a trump is returned? You are going down in a cold contract.

"The expert line is to win the ♡A and return a low heart immediately. You win the return, ruff a low heart with the ♠K and draw trumps. Subsequently your carefully preserved ♡K will provide you with trick twelve."

"Nicely played Professor. Lose 13 IMPs." said Ross sardonically. "My teammate also made the safety play, which was just as well since RHO held all four spades and a singleton heart. But Mercilla made all thirteen tricks and what's more, she and Flavia bid the grand slam! Now what do you think?"

"How did they ever bid a grand slam on those cards?" croaked Professor Silver hoarsely.

"They employ a convention called the Eastwood Asking Bid — an unusual jump in the trump suit which asks partner how lucky she feels. Here is how the auction went..."

FLAVIA
- ♠ K 3
- ♡ 6 5
- ◇ 10 9 5 3
- ♣ Q 8 5 3 2

KHEDIVE
- ♠ —
- ♡ Q J 10 9 8 3
- ◇ Q J
- ♣ A K J 10 4

ROSS
- ♠ 8 7 5 4
- ♡ 4
- ◇ 8 7 6 4 2
- ♣ 9 7 6

```
  N
W   E
  S
```

MERCILLA
- ♠ A Q J 10 9 6 2
- ♡ A K 7 2
- ◇ A K
- ♣ —

West	North	East	South
KHEDIVE	FLAVIA	ROSS	MERCILLA
			2♣
pass	2◇	pass	2♠
pass	5♠[1]	pass	6♣[2]
pass	7♠[3]	all pass	

1. Eastwood ('Well, do you feel lucky, partner?')
2. Eastwood Corollary ('No, but do you?')
3. Yes!

"The opening lead was the ♡Q which Mercilla won with her ace. Any normal player would now cash the ♡K and attempt to ruff two hearts in dummy, a line that obviously fails here. But not this declarer! She played the ◇A and ◇K, felling my partner's doubleton QJ ! Then she crossed to the ♠K, my partner showing out, and played out the ◇10 and ◇9 discarding her two heart losers as I helplessly followed suit. A small spade to her hand enabled her to draw my trumps and claim the contract."

Professor Silver was not amused. He motioned Ross to continue.

"All my remaining doubts vanished when late in the match I made a lead-directing double. The bidding had gone:

West	North	East	South
KHEDIVE	FLAVIA	ROSS	MERCILLA
	1♣	pass	1◇
pass	2◇	pass	4◇¹
pass	4♠²	dbl	7◇
all pass			

1. Eastwood ('Well, do you feel lucky, partner?')
2. Positive response

"I held the ace and king of spades, hence my double of the four spade bid. Mercilla had no vestige of a spade control, yet, fully confident in their system, bid the grand slam anyway. And what do you think happened?"

We both held our breath, waiting for the punch line.

"My poor partner found himself on lead, with a spade void! Without a spade lead, Mercilla was able to draw trumps, and discard her spades on dummy's clubs. Seven diamonds bid and made!"

Ross was unable to continue and after a few minutes rest, took his leave of us.

"These are much deeper waters than I had thought, Cardinal," muttered Silver, in a voice so low I could hardly make out his words. In all the years that I have been playing bridge, I have heard of only one similar instance, the infamous Voodoo Dummy Case that occurred at the 1934 Haitian Championships. I was on the appeals committee, but the matter was left unresolved after hand-carved dolls resembling each of the committee members were found on the beach. We must prepare ourselves for tomorrow night. There is but one step from the grotesque to the horrible. Tomorrow morning, go to the local market and buy a sack of garlic, three dozen stalks of wolfbane, and four crucifixes. Speak to no-one of this matter, especially neither Bruce nor Eric."

"Surely, Professor, you who will not even condescend to watch *The X-Files*, don't believe that there is anything other than blind luck involved here, do you?"

"Cardinal, how often have I said to you that when you have eliminated the impossible, whatever remains, however improbable, must be the truth? Well, there's nothing to be done until tomorrow morning. You get some sleep while I think. This is definitely a three-pipe problem. And by the way..."

"Yes, Professor?"

"When you go out tomorrow, do not consort with any friendly young women you might chance to encounter. The term 'necking' has a different connotation in Ruritania than it does in Canada!"

The Ruritanian Falcon

"We've got to have a fall guy," said Professor Silver. "Bruce will be back soon and we have to break it to him that we lost the match. We need someone to take the heat."

"Surely, David," Eric Murray began, "you, as captain, should take the rap? After all, you've been explaining lost matches to Gowdy for thirty-five years and it was your decision to switch partners for the last set...."

"I can't," said Professor Silver earnestly. "I won't. I mean it." He sat up straight. A pleasant smile illuminated his face, momentarily erasing the wrinkles. "Listen to me, guys, I'm telling you what's best for all of us. If we don't feed Bruce a fall guy, it's ten to one he'll eat us *all* raw. Sure, I've had to apologize once or twice over the years, but he was always right there at the table so losing came as no surprise. This is different: when he was called away he thought we had the match locked up! Soon he'll be walking into this room expecting to find us celebrating; then we'll have to duck for cover!"

"Aw, come on, Professor," said Wright Cardinal, "we can handle him. Remember how he just laughed when you didn't overcall your nine-card spade suit that time? I thought he would be over the table at you, and that was a Spingold match you blew. Besides, I'm willing to tell him, he likes me."

"Show me how you're going to calm him down, and I'll go along," said Silver. "I'll go along with anything but I need to be persuaded there's a fifty-fifty chance of getting out of this room alive. You've got to convince me that you know what you're doing and not simply fooling around by guess and by God, hoping it'll all come out right somehow in the end. Well? No? How about you, Eric, got any ideas? You neither? Well, I do: let's give him Mia!"

Mia Culpa moved away from Professor Silver and twisted herself down on the sofa. Her face was open-mouthed, open-eyed, greenish, and amazed. She struggled for breath and finally began to sob as tears rolled down her cheeks.

"You're right. I'm sorry I was such a lousy kibitzer. I certainly didn't bring you any luck. I know it's all my fault, I chatter and distract everyone, but that Mercilla woman kept talking to me. You guys get out of here; I'll stay and I'll ......" her words faded into inaudible moans.

Eric Murray tightened the corners of his mouth in what may have been a minute smile; Professor Silver's proposal seemed to have no other effect on him. Wright Cardinal, after a lengthy pause, finally spoke.

"It won't fly, Professor. I know what you're thinking and you're right: Bruce wouldn't raise his voice to a woman, let alone his fist. She'd be the perfect victim. But we can't pin it on her — all she did was play the dummy for the last hand when Bruce had to leave. Besides, to put her under the gun after she flew 4000 miles to cheer us on seems pretty shabby."

"All she did was play the dummy? All she did was ask Princess Flavia if she *was* really out of spades! I might have made three notrumps redoubled if the revoke had been established and we wouldn't be on the spot now! But if you don't want to do that, do you have any better ideas?"

"Let's give him Wright," suggested Murray, unexpectedly.

Professor Silver remained still and expressionless for a long moment. Then he said "By God, Eric, you're a character. You really are. There's never any telling what you'll do or say next, except it's bound to be something astonishing." He began to laugh.

"There's nothing funny about it. He said it himself: Bruce does like him *and* he respects his bridge ability. Probably the whole thing will pass quietly."

"But my dear man," Silver objected, "can't you see? If I even for a moment thought of doing it — but that's ridiculous, I feel towards Cardinal as if he were my own grandson, I really do — but if I even for a moment thought of doing what you propose, what in the world would we tell Bruce that would convince him that it's all Wright's fault?"

"Simply that Wright misplayed three notrumps and we ended up losing by 3 IMPs!"

"Well, Eric, if you're really serious about this, er, suggestion of yours, the least we can do in common politeness is to hear you out. Now, just how are you going to explain our loss to Bruce," Professor Silver paused here to laugh again, "so that he won't dismember us and throw our body parts into the Danube?"

"It was board 12. Wright opened one notrump and I raised him to three. You remember the hand, don't you?"

MURRAY
♠ A 6 4
♡ Q 10 5
♢ A 3 2
♣ 6 5 4 3

ALUCARD		RENFREW
♠ J 10 7 2		♠ Q 9 8
♡ A J 7 3	N	♡ 8 6
♢ Q 7	W E	♢ J 9 8 5
♣ 9 8 2	S	♣ Q J 10 7

CARDINAL
♠ K 5 3
♡ K 9 4 2
♢ K 10 6 4
♣ A K

"At the other table against the same contract, you led a small heart from your AJxx, which was a disaster for us. But a heart was a reasonable lead from the West hand so we won't charge you for the game swing. Wright, however, saw the deuce of spades hit the table. He won the ♠A in his hand and began well by playing a small heart to dummy's ten, which held. Then he called for the ♢A from the dummy, to which both opponents followed with a small spot. At this point Wright had eight tricks: two spades, two hearts, two diamonds, and the ♣AK. What would you do next, Professor?"

"Why, precisely what Cardinal did: I would make the technically correct play of another diamond to the ten. It is obvious from the opening lead that spades are 4-3, so if either red suit splits three-three, I can arrive at nine tricks. Meanwhile, I have the extra chance that East started with both the queen and jack of diamonds. LHO wins this trick, and we can safely win the inevitable spade return and drive out the ♡A. Unfortunately, as I recall the exact layout on this hand, neither red suit breaks, there are no squeezes or endplays, and Wright naturally went one down. What's your point, Eric?"

"The diamond suit, that's my point. Let's look at it again.

A 3 2

K 10 6 4

If Wright had been playing the final of the Bermuda Bowl, his play would have been picture perfect. Technically, his play of the ◇A followed by a low diamond to the ten gives him his best chance of making three tricks from the suit — a total probability of 56%.

"But, my dear professor, we do not make our plays in the laboratory, we make them at the bridge table against real opponents, who are fallible. Surely in this case, your RHO is a player who will almost certainly split his honours from QJxx, and this changes the odds dramatically: no longer do they favour playing the ◇10 by a 3-2 factor. On the contrary, when East plays low on the second diamond, you should win your king, trying to drop a doubleton honour in the West hand, then lead another heart up to dummy's queen.

"West cannot afford to rise with the ♡A or you have nine tricks, so now you are in dummy to play another diamond towards the ten. If West turns out to have four diamonds and four hearts along with his four spades, you will still go down, but this is virtually the only lie of the cards that can defeat you. Wright took a reasonable line, but he forgot to play the opponents as well as the cards, and guess what — the ◇Q *was* doubleton on his left! *He's* our fall guy."

"You lousy, two-bit shyster," snarled Wright Cardinal. "You're the one who blew the match. Now there's no prize money and no plane ticket. How am I going to get home?"

"In a box, most likely," quipped the irrepressible Silver, "unless we can figure something out before Bruce gets here. But how was it Eric's fault that we lost?"

"He let the opponents make three notrumps, that's how!" Scribbling furiously, Wright showed them board # 22.

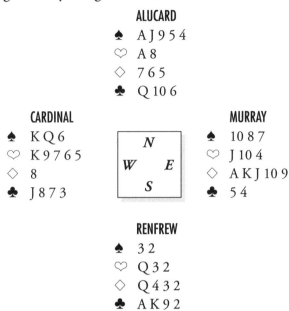

ALUCARD
♠ A J 9 5 4
♡ A 8
♢ 7 6 5
♣ Q 10 6

CARDINAL
♠ K Q 6
♡ K 9 7 6 5
♢ 8
♣ J 8 7 3

MURRAY
♠ 10 8 7
♡ J 10 4
♢ A K J 10 9
♣ 5 4

RENFREW
♠ 3 2
♡ Q 3 2
♢ Q 4 3 2
♣ A K 9 2

"Eric opened a weak two bid in diamonds, and Renfrew ended up as declarer in 3NT. I led the ♢8, Eric won and shifted to the ♡J. Declarer played low from his hand and won dummy's ace. Renfrew then crossed to the ♣A and played a spade. I played low, hoping that he would finesse the nine, but he played the jack, followed by ace and another. Endplayed, I tried a heart, but declarer was able to get a count on the hand and play the clubs for no losers, making four."

"Essentially what happened at our table," said the professor. "I don't see what else Eric could have done, but if you think we can pin our loss on him I'm perfectly willing to discuss it with you."

"If, instead of hoping my hearts were good enough to set 3NT, Eric had continued with the ♢A and ♢J, I would have discarded my ♠KQ. Now declarer can't run spades without letting Eric in with the ♠10! Renfrew can only come to four club tricks (if he takes a first-round finesse with dummy's ten), two spades, one heart, and the ♢Q —

eight tricks. That's one down, 9 IMPs to us and we win the match."

Professor Silver laughed, a harsh exultant snort. Eric, however, said calmly "Come now, gentlemen, let's keep our discussion on a friendly basis. There certainly seems to be something in what Wright says, but before pronouncing sentence on me, perhaps you should look at the evidence. You may then be forced to reconsider your verdict."

"If I defend as Wright wants me to, think carefully about the position after South wins the ◇Q at trick three. Sami Kehela would claim! You don't see it? Declarer simply cashes dummy's two major suit aces and plays ♣Q, ♣A, and ♣K. A 3-3 club break would lead to an even quicker squeeze and endplay on my hand, but since that doesn't happen, declarer now plays his deuce of clubs. I have to make two pitches on the clubs, and for now I can spare my two last hearts, no problem. But now Wright is on lead with only hearts left.

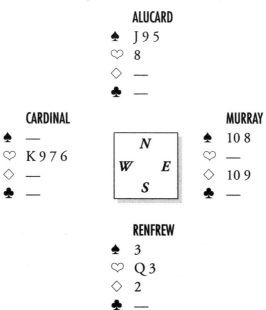

ALUCARD
♠ J 9 5
♡ 8
◇ —
♣ —

CARDINAL   **MURRAY**

♠ —   ♠ 10 8
♡ K 9 7 6   ♡ —
◇ —   ◇ 10 9
♣ —   ♣ —

RENFREW
♠ 3
♡ Q 3
◇ 2
♣ —

"If he cashes the king and exits to Renfrew's queen, I'm squeezed: if I throw a spade, dummy is high, and if I throw two diamonds, the deuce in declarer's hand becomes trick nine. Cardinal can make a try by leading a low heart instead of the king, but again I have to shed a diamond so all Renfrew has to do is win and exit with the deuce of diamonds. I win our fourth and last trick and have to lead from my ♠10 into dummy's ♠J9 tenace. Squeezed or endplayed, take your pick: the contract can't be beaten."

"Nice try, Cardinal," said Professor Silver, nodding in agreement, "but you're still on the hook."

There was a loud knock at the door. Wright put his hands to his face and uttered a short strangled cry. "It's Bruce," he whimpered.

"Take it easy, you coward," said Professor Silver as he strode to the door. "Bruce wouldn't bother to knock. See, it's just the bellboy with a parcel for me."

Curiosity overcame fear as every eye was riveted on the oblong box in Professor Silver's hands. He placed it on the table, opened it, and unwrapped a small statuette which had been swaddled in towels. It was a small bird, made of a dull, gray-coloured metal, with wings outspread, talons open, just as if it were swooping down on its prey. Inscribed on the base was, THE LILY KEY MEMORIAL TROPHY, AWARDED TO THE PLAYER MAKING THE MOST COSTLY MISTAKE OF THE RURITANIAN GRAND CHAMPIONSHIP. 1995 WINNER, PROFESSOR DAVID S. SILVER. POUR LE MÉRITE.

"What's that?" asked Wright, managing an air of innocence.

"Oh, that? It appears to be a replica of a Ruritanian falcon, a small indigenous bird that lives in the mountains. Eats rats as I recall. Nice example of local handicrafts; I'll just put it away in my room."

"Not so fast, Professor," intervened Eric with a malevolent smile. "Perhaps you can enlighten us as to what feat of stupidity you performed for the committee to award you this token of their esteem."

"This is obviously a joke. I was double-dummy for the whole match. You don't believe me? Well then, I ask you to consider Bruce's exact words when he screamed at me tonight."

"But Bruce didn't scream at you tonight," said Wright.

"Exactly! I couldn't have made even a small blunder without Bruce's going ballistic at the top of his lungs. A catastrophic error would have brought a response that would have broken the sound barrier! This is obviously the work of the Hentzau family — they have never forgiven my father for fighting on the wrong side during the Franco-Prussian war."

"Oh, but you're wrong, Professor," said Mia, a malevolent gleam in her eyes. "Bruce had left the room for the last hand and I was playing the dummy. That's why he never said anything. It was your fascination with that Mercilla that caused you to misplay it."

"Mia — why are you doing this to me after all the time we've spent at the table together?"

"Listen, Professor. This isn't a damned bit of good. You'll never understand, but I'll try once and then we'll give it up. Listen. When your partner gets framed you have to do something about it, it doesn't make any difference what he thinks of you. Wright was my partner for two years and I'm supposed to do something about it. When a bridge player takes a bum rap it's bad business to let the guilty person get away with it. It's bad for that player, and it's bad for every bridge player everywhere.

"Sure, I was paying cash for every session Wright sat opposite me, but at least he was polite and tried to teach me something about the game. Not like you, professor — you just played with me to feed your ego on my insecurities. No, *you* screwed up that last hand and you're going over for it.

"Look, guys, here's the hand:

GOWDY
- ♠ Q 6 5
- ♡ Q 6 5 4
- ◇ A 8
- ♣ J 10 5 4

SILVER
- ♠ A K
- ♡ A 9
- ◇ Q 9 7 6 5 4 3
- ♣ A Q

"Professor Silver opened 1◇, Mr. Gowdy bid 1♡, and Professor Silver jumped to 3NT, doubled by Mercilla on his left and redoubled by the Professor. The opening lead was the ♠J and it was at this moment that Bruce was summoned to take a transatlantic conference call. He walked behind Professor Silver, looked at his hand, glanced at the dummy, and left smiling. Declarer won the ♠A and tabled the ◇3. Mercilla took a deep breath and leaned forward to peer at the ◇3, then followed slowly with the deuce. Enchanted by the view, our bridge 'expert' carelessly called for dummy's ace, and Princess Flavia played a small heart!

"Sweating profusely, Professor Silver attempted to establish dummy's clubs while the ♠Q remained intact. He played the ♣A, and then the ♣Q, which held the trick! He exited with a diamond, won on his left and found himself back in his hand when another spade was led at him. Another diamond exit and dummy's ♠Q stopped that suit for the last time, as Princess Flavia played a small club. Dummy's ♣J was played, won on his right as he shed a diamond and Mercilla followed. A low heart was tabled; Professor Silver looked at it for a long time and finally played low from his hand. Mercilla grabbed her ♡K, cashed two more spades and gave up. Three down redoubled, vulnerable, in an ice-cold contract! Yes, I think Mr. Gowdy would have vocalized his chagrin had he been at the table."

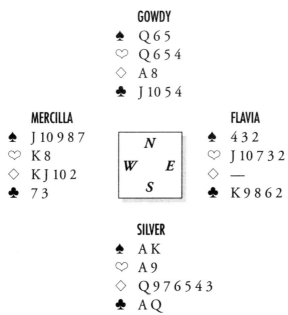

GOWDY
♠ Q 6 5
♡ Q 6 5 4
◇ A 8
♣ J 10 5 4

MERCILLA
♠ J 10 9 8 7
♡ K 8
◇ K J 10 2
♣ 7 3

FLAVIA
♠ 4 3 2
♡ J 10 7 3 2
◇ —
♣ K 9 8 6 2

SILVER
♠ A K
♡ A 9
◇ Q 9 7 6 5 4 3
♣ A Q

Professor Silver's long-held smile had become a dreadful grimace. He remained silent as Mia continued.

"If you had given the hand a moment's thought you might have wondered why that peroxide blonde doubled. Obviously she thought her partner was on lead and wanted a diamond through! But even without that elementary deduction you should have seen that only a four-zero diamond split offside could set the contract. All you had to do was play dummy's $\diamond$8.

"If East won, the suit was splitting no worse than 3-1. You win any return and cash the $\diamond$A. If both opponents follow, the suit splits and you can claim. If an opponent shows out, you cross to your hand with the $\clubsuit$A, refusing the finesse, and drive out the last diamond. The hand is unbeatable, except when played by a geriatric voyeur."

"Wow! Thanks, Mia," exclaimed a now cheerful Cardinal. "But tell me — how come you're suddenly such a great analyst?"

"Don't be too sure I'm as bad a player as I'm supposed to be: that kind of reputation is awfully good for lulling opponents into overbidding. I could see this coming right after Mercilla found herself on lead. She leaned forward, smiled at him, and the championship was lost. No, Professor," she pointed accusingly at the wretched man, "you played the sap and you're going over for it."

"Time to go," muttered the professor. He picked up his trophy and turned to leave, just as Bruce Gowdy entered the hotel room.

"Hi, Dave, is that the big trophy you have there?" he asked genially, pointing to the statuette.

"No, Bruce," replied Silver sadly. "I'm afraid it's the stuff that nightmares are made of....."

RECTIFYING THE COUNT

It is with a heavy heart that I take up my pen to write the last words in which I shall ever record the singular gifts by which my friend Professor David Silver was distinguished. In an incoherent and, as I deeply feel, an entirely inadequate fashion, I have endeavoured to give some account of my experiences as his bridge associate from the chance which first brought us together at the period of *'A Study in Silver'* up to the time of our ill-fated trip to Ruritania.

It was my intention to chronicle our exploits at the Ruritanian Invitational Team Championships and to stop there and to have said nothing of subsequent events. My hand has been forced, however, by the recent letters to various prestigious bridge journals in which Count Alucard defends the memory of his protegé, and I have no choice but to lay the facts before the bridge-playing public exactly as they occurred. I alone know the absolute truth of the matter, and I am satisfied that the time has come when no good purpose is served by its suppression. It lies with me to tell for the first time what really took place between Mercilla Fortuna and Professor Silver in the bowels of Castle Zelda.

After our loss to Count Alucard's team, Professor Silver and I were stranded in Streslau without sufficient funds to return to Toronto. I was in the depths of despair since I was committed to playing in the Summer Nationals with three clients whose continued patronage was essential to my livelihood. Professor Silver, however, was steeped in lethargy and had scarcely stirred for a week. It was not in his nature to take an aimless holiday, and something about his pale, worn face told me that his nerves were at their highest tension. He saw the question in my eyes, and, putting his finger-tips together and his elbows on his knees, he explained the situation.

"You have never before heard of Count Alucard?" said he.

"Never, before this last event."

"There's the genius and the danger of the thing!" he cried. "The man pervades the bridge world, and no one has heard of him. I tell you Cardinal, in all seriousness, that if I could free bridge of that man, I should feel that my own career had reached its summit, and I should be prepared to turn to some more placid line in life. But I could not rest, Cardinal, I could not sit quiet in my chair, if I thought such a fiend as Count Alucard was sitting at a bridge table unchallenged."

"But what has he done?"

"He is the organizer of half that is evil and of nearly all that is undetected in our great game. He sits motionless, like a spider in the centre of his web, but he does little himself. He only plans. But his agents are numerous and splendidly controlled. Is there a match to be stolen, a bottom board to be apportioned, a championship snatched from a grasp — Alucard gives an order and the matter is carried out. His agent may be exposed and reviled, but the central power which uses the agent is never caught — never so much as suspected. This is the evil that I deduced, Cardinal, and which I came to Ruritania to extinguish."

"But who are these agents of whom you speak?"

"Not 'who', Cardinal, 'what'! Count Alucard's agents are legendary monsters known in bridge clubs here as the 'Un-Players'. Dismissed in the West as a primitive myth, the Un-Players lurk in tournaments, ready to pounce on their unsuspecting prey. I had read about them, of course, but I never believed they existed until I investigated the strange case of Orlando Whiffle. Oh, come now, you know Whiffle. He's a player who can barely follow suit, has the attention span of a fruit fly and yet wins hundreds of master points every year. One evening, he fell asleep while playing a grand slam and his cravat slipped. To my horror, I saw twin canine punctures on his neck, the mark of the Un-Player. I spent the next few months examining the necks of certain opponents — you may recall the unpleasantness that ensued when Midge Griffin misunderstood my intentions during a match; so far I have identified three of them in our local duplicate club alone."

"Silver, this is monstrous! But tell me, how does he transform them into good bridge players?"

"Not into good bridge players — winning bridge players. No evil alchemy can change an untalented card pusher into a real bridge player. No, they maintain whatever level of ability they had when they offered up their jugulars to him. He seduces them with the promise of winning without acquiring skill, of success without effort, of bushels of masterpoints for simply showing up at the table. He accomplishes this by convincing them that they are lucky, that luck will overcome superior opponents, that luck can be substituted for hard work, study, and practice; in short, he teaches them the Lots of Luck bidding system."

"But, Professor, most bridge tournaments are two-session events: how would an Un-Player manage to attend afternoon sessions?"

"Ah, you see, contrary to popular belief, the light of the sun does not destroy Un-Players, it merely substantially diminishes their powers. How often have we heard bridge players complain that they have great games in the afternoon sessions only to suffer meltdown in the evening? It is not fatigue which robs them of victory, but the intensity of the supernatural forces newly aligned against them.

"And there is a very practical reason why Un-Players are attracted to bridge. As a result of the physical deterioration which bridge players suffer, owing to their sedentary life style and appalling dietary habits, humans and Un-Players are virtually indistinguishable at the table."

"But Professor! What does this imply for our rubber bridge match against Alucard and Mercilla tonight? I had hoped we could win enough money to buy a plane ticket home. Maybe we should wear crucifixes and chew garlic again? "

"No, as we discovered to our cost in the final of the tournament, that's yet another example of inept research by that charlatan, Van Helsing, which has been accepted by a gullible public. Religious symbols serve only to keep an Un-Player at least two feet from the wearer, insufficient to protect you at the bridge table. Garlic is slightly more effective, as its aroma may compel an Un-Player to leave a room immediately; unfortunately it usually has the same effect on everyone else.

"But don't despair, Cardinal, I have thought of a way of nullifying the powers of our opponents. By all means, let us away to Castle Zelda tonight. All you have to do is play well, and not question anything I say."

"Welcome, gentlemen, to Castle Zelda," said Count Alucard, baring his fangs amicably. "Won't you try a glass of the local vintage? The grapes come from my own vineyard."

"I never drink wine," said the professor, to my astonishment. "I will, however, take some wild rose tea if you have some, which I doubt."

"You know too much, von Zelber," snarled our host. "Let's get on with our game, shall we?"

Atypically, Professor Silver and I were substantially ahead when the critical part of the match began just as the clock struck midnight. Mercilla opened the bidding with one notrump, and a normal Un-Player auction unfolded:

West	North	East	South
SILVER	ALUCARD	CARDINAL	MERCILLA
pass	pass	pass	1NT
pass	3♣[1]	pass	3NT[2]
all pass			

1. Eastwood — do you feel lucky?
2. Acceptance; normal for Mercilla about 90% of the time

As anyone who knew him would expect, Professor Silver led a heart.

```
                    ALUCARD
               ♠  7 6
               ♡  Q 4
               ◇  Q 8 5
               ♣  A J 9 6 4 3

                              CARDINAL
                         ♠  K 10 5 2
         ┌─────────┐     ♡  10 8 2
         │    N    │     ◇  K 10 9 4
         │  W   E  │     ♣  10 2
         │    S    │
         └─────────┘
```

Mercilla rose with dummy's queen while I followed low after contemplating the dummy and my hand.

Mercilla immediately called for a low club, playing the king from her hand, and Professor Silver followed smoothly with the queen. Furrowing her brow, Mercilla inexplicably tranced for a few minutes and finally produced a low diamond. Smiling coquettishly at Professor Silver when he followed low, she confidently called for dummy's queen. I won the trick with my king, and returned the ♡10 which held. Another heart lead from me drew the king from declarer and the ace from Professor Silver, who then cashed two more hearts for one down!

"Dammit!" said Mercilla uneasily. "The cards were certainly placed badly."

"On the contrary," said Professor Silver, "the only card that mattered was onside: I held queen-third of clubs."

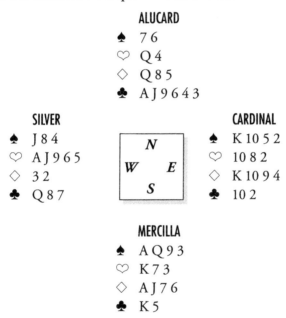

ALUCARD
♠ 7 6
♡ Q 4
◇ Q 8 5
♣ A J 9 6 4 3

SILVER
♠ J 8 4
♡ A J 9 6 5
◇ 3 2
♣ Q 8 7

CARDINAL
♠ K 10 5 2
♡ 10 8 2
◇ K 10 9 4
♣ 10 2

MERCILLA
♠ A Q 9 3
♡ K 7 3
◇ A J 7 6
♣ K 5

"When I dropped the ♣Q under your king, you assumed that it was a singleton, and that it would therefore be impossible to establish the suit without surrendering the lead to Cardinal's presumed ten-fourth. A heart return through your king would, as we have seen, set the contract. As I anticipated, you switched to the diamond suit as your primary source of tricks. Of course, the ◇K onside is not enough in itself — you also needed the suit to split 3-3; but suits always divide favourably for you, don't they, Countess? But there you were, 'a pauper in the midst of wealth', with nine top tricks waiting to be cashed."

Mercilla became uncharacteristically silent as Professor Silver and I won the next two rubbers handily. But, after leaving the room briefly to take nourishment, she perked up and soon landed in another vulnerable game. Once again, success depended upon a lucky lie of cards to bring in dummy's long suit.

West	North	East	South
SILVER	ALUCARD	CARDINAL	MERCILLA
			1♣
pass	1◇	pass	1NT
pass	3◇[1]	pass	3NT[2]
all pass			

1. Eastwood — do you feel lucky?
2. Of course

Professor Silver led the ♡K and a surprisingly strong dummy contributed the ace to the first trick:

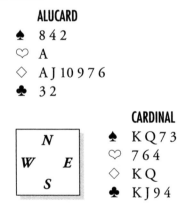

ALUCARD
♠ 8 4 2
♡ A
◇ A J 10 9 7 6
♣ 3 2

CARDINAL
♠ K Q 7 3
♡ 7 6 4
◇ K Q
♣ K J 9 4

The contract seemed Mercilla-proof, since, as usual, most of the outstanding high cards were well-placed. The clubs were all under declarer, and the diamond position filled me with a sense of impending doom. Accustomed as she was to her finesses always working, Mercilla played a club to her queen and didn't even bother to wait for Professor Silver to follow with a low club before leading a small diamond to dummy's ten. I won this with the ◇K and returned the ♡4 to my partner's ♡8. He exited with a spade, which went to my queen and Mercilla's ace, and she confidently played another diamond to the jack. I won the ◇Q and returned my last heart to the Professor's ten, then watched him cash two more hearts. Declarer was thunderstruck. She looked up at her partner with tears in her eyes.

"What's happening, Vladimir? All I needed was a three-two diamond split with one honour onside — but they were both offside. The contract couldn't be made."

"Let me rephrase that for you, my dear Countess," Professor Silver said malevolently. "Instead of 'the contract couldn't be made' you should have said '*I* couldn't make the contract'. The contract is in fact unbeatable due to an extraordinarily fortunate lie of the cards. You failed because you took a zero percentage play in the diamond suit instead of anticipating the only position in which you could succeed."

"Nonsense!" interjected Count Alucard, with some heat. "The probability of the double finesse's succeeding is 75% and the suit will split 3-2 68% of the time giving a total probability of more than 50%!"

"Sir, control yourself! No purpose is served by getting emotional. Let us look at the entire hand, and reflect, if you will, on whom you are playing against. On the face of it, your partner is right about her chances. But you are playing against experts and you must expect an expert defence. With no dummy entries outside the diamond suit, I put it to you that if Cardinal and I are defending there is no way you can bring home AJ10xxx opposite two little for five tricks when the honours are split and the suit is dividing 3-2. When you take your first finesse, neither of us will contribute an honour; you will win that trick, and later the ace, but that's all. Even if both honours are onside the play will go the same way.

"No, the only real hope is to play for a doubleton KQ in either hand, the situation that actually existed! Duck the first trick entirely, then play the ace when you regain the lead — and five diamond tricks are yours. You know, there's really no point in being lucky if you can't recognize a felicitous situation when you see one."

The next few hands were played out in an ominous silence, broken only by the occasional sniffle from the Countess Fortuna. It was as we were finishing what all had agreed would be the final rubber, that the now infamous hand came up.

It began innocently enough. Mercilla opened the bidding with 1♠, my partner passed, Count Alucard bid 2♢ and Mercilla bid a firm 2♠. Alucard continued with 3♣, and Mercilla, after some thought, bid 3NT. Her partner considered this for some time, finally emerging from his trance with a call of 5NT. Mercilla alerted, then looked confused, cancelled the alert, and then alerted again. The professor and I gazed impassively at her as she finally produced a bid of 6NT, which ended the tortured sequence. Silver led the ♠J, the dummy was put down, and we defended the slam.

ALUCARD
♠ K
♡ Q 5
♢ A K J 10 5
♣ K Q J 10 5

SILVER
♠ J 10
♡ K 10 8 2
♢ Q 8 7 4 2
♣ A 3

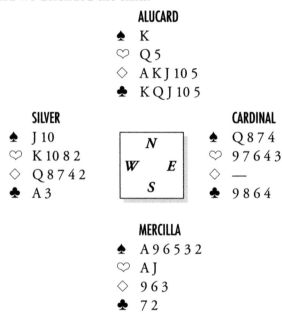

CARDINAL
♠ Q 8 7 4
♡ 9 7 6 4 3
♢ —
♣ 9 8 6 4

MERCILLA
♠ A 9 6 5 3 2
♡ A J
♢ 9 6 3
♣ 7 2

Declarer looked pleasantly surprised to find herself in quite a good contract, one that would require little more than a routine diamond finesse to bring home. Winning the ♠K, she cashed the ♢A, and was horrified to see me contribute a small heart to this trick. Visibly shaken, she called for the ♣K, which Silver won; the professor exited with his ♣3, and the Countess was once again in dummy.

Her only chance now for twelve tricks, it appeared, was to find me with the ♡K, but it was not to be. Mercilla seemed almost to expect it now when her ♡J lost, and yet another promising hand had ended up in the minus column.

"Bad luck, my dear," Alucard said solicitously. "It's just one of those hands that can't be made."

"It is always a mistake to propose theories without examining the facts," said Professor Silver. "It is in fact a typically lucky hand. All you need is the ♡K on your *left* and the hand is cold."

"That's enough!" cried Alucard, rising to his feet. "I've had all I can take of your condescending pedantry, Professor. Would you care to put your money where your mouth is? You are up a few thousand dollars — perhaps you would like to wager double or nothing you can make twelve tricks against a spade lead?"

"Indeed," replied Silver to my horror. I protested, but there was nothing for it but to replay the hand with Silver as declarer.

"Once again," he began, "we find the charming Countess adopting a line that against expert defenders could never succeed, instead of taking advantage of a fortuitous lie of cards that allowed her to make her contract. Observe the situation after I have discovered the diamond position, knocked out the ♣A, and been put back in dummy.

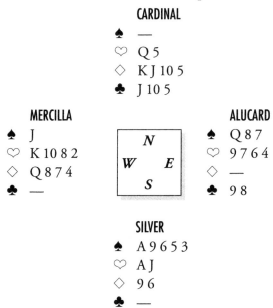

CARDINAL
♠ —
♡ Q 5
◇ K J 10 5
♣ J 10 5

MERCILLA
♠ J
♡ K 10 8 2
◇ Q 8 7 4
♣ —

ALUCARD
♠ Q 8 7
♡ 9 7 6 4
◇ —
♣ 9 8

SILVER
♠ A 9 6 5 3
♡ A J
◇ 9 6
♣ —

"This hand is much more subtle than it seems, since finding the ♡K with East will not actually help declarer. On the surface, of course, there would be twelve tricks — four diamonds (by leading the nine from hand), four clubs, two spades, and two hearts. Once again, however, the Countess forgot the calibre of her opposition. An alert East would put up the ♡K on a low heart lead from dummy, and declarer would be doomed. If she cashed the ♠A after winning her ♡A, what in the world would she throw from dummy? No matter which diamond she chose, she would be unable to gather more than three diamond tricks without a second finesse, for which there is no means of transport. Suddenly, the trick total is reduced to eleven.

"It is critical, therefore, that the heart suit, playing its accustomed pivotal role, afford declarer not just two tricks, *but two entries,* in order to be able to cash the ♠A *after* the diamond plays. Yet, surely, the doughty Cardinal would have had no difficulty making such a routine play as the ♡K?

"So you must think more deeply about the hand, since your only hope is indeed that the ♡K is favourably placed — with West! I shall demonstrate: I play out dummy's clubs, and then lead the ♡Q off dummy, overtaking with the ♡A, and reaching this ending:

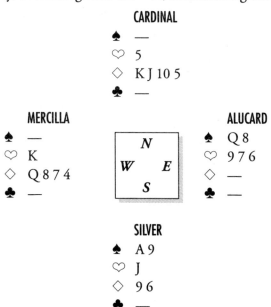

CARDINAL
♠ —
♡ 5
◇ K J 10 5
♣ —

MERCILLA
♠ —
♡ K
◇ Q 8 7 4
♣ —

ALUCARD
♠ Q 8
♡ 9 7 6
◇ —
♣ —

SILVER
♠ A 9
♡ J
◇ 9 6
♣ —

"When I lead the ♠A the Countess cannot afford to part with a diamond, for then I shall discard dummy's heart and lead the ◇9, making the rest of the tricks. Never one to embarrass a lady, I might point out her alternative, which is to jettison the long-preserved ♡K. But alas, the age of chivalry is past. I no longer need the ◇5 in dummy: I simply play a diamond to the ten, return to my hand with the ♡J, and repeat the diamond finesse for my twelfth trick.

"A charming paradox — the slam is cold with the ♡K offside, and impossible with it onside. My Bridge 101 students used to encounter something very similar in week five, in a homework exercise from Ottlik and Kelsey's well-known text. A very lucky hand, of course, but it takes a skilful declarer to recognize the situation and play for the winning ending."

"No, Mercilla! Stop!" screamed Alucard as Mercilla reached across the table and grabbed Professor Silver. He struggled briefly, but she was much too strong for him to escape. Before anyone could intervene she sank her fangs into his throat and drank deeply from his jugular vein.

It was a scene from nightmare and the details of what happened afterwards are not clear in my memory, but I know for a certainty that three events occurred in rapid succession: Mercilla fell to the ground dead, Professor Silver sat down smiling, and I fainted.

I awoke to a strange humming noise in my ears. After a moment's reflection I realized that I was listening to the sound of jet engines, and, opening my eyes, I perceived that I was seated in the first class cabin of an Air Canada 747. Pinned to my shirt was an envelope addressed to me. I opened it and read:

My dear Cardinal (it said)

> *I write these few lines to allay your fears both for my safety and for your own financial well-being. As to the first, we were never in any serious danger. A real bridge player's blood is 80% caffeine, a poison that in that quantity is sufficient to kill a small bull. My own blood in addition contains a substantial concentration of nicotine, an even stronger poison; poor Countess Fortuna died instantly.*
>
> *I am pleased to think that my forthcoming monograph,*

'Defensive Methods Against Extraordinarily Lucky Opponents', *will free bridge from the further predations of Count Alucard's agents. Luck is based on confidence and the key is to point out remorselessly every mistake they make. It will take some discipline, since bridge players are by nature kind and considerate, but I am sure that we shall all do what must be done. The Un-Players will be restricted to a diet of novices and amateurs, who are in any case their lawful prey.*

I have transferred our winnings to your bank account in Toronto; you should have sufficient money to support you until the Summer Nationals. As for me, His Majesty has appointed me to the position of Official Dummy to the Court. My duties are always to place His Majesty in a contract he can make, and always to put down a dummy strong enough to justify his bidding. After thirty-five years of partnering Bruce Gowdy, neither of these tasks should present a problem.

Pray give my greetings to all my friends in the bridge world, and believe me to be, my dear fellow, very sincerely yours.

Professor David Silver (retired)